Smart Specialisation

"I commend Professor Dominique Foray for making this book available to the wide community of economic scholars and policy-makers, as it will surely foster the development of ever more refined policy ideas along the lines of *Smart Specialisation.*"

Manuel Trajtenberg, Professor at the Eitan Berglas School of Economics, Tel Aviv University, Israel

This is the first book on a new policy approach that has been widely adopted in Europe and beyond. It analyses the concept of smart specialisation, discusses the need for smart specialisation strategies, explains why the approach is new and different from more standard policy processes and explores the conditions for successful implementation.

Smart Specialisation: Opportunities and Challenges for Regional Innovation Policy describes the origin of the concept, explains when a smart specialisation policy is necessary, provides a detailed analysis of the design principles of the policy and discusses the pertinence of this approach according to regional development levels. Finally the book takes into consideration the practical implementation phase of the process based on initial feedback acquired from regions engaged in the preparation of their smart specialisation strategy.

The book is original in that it provides the first full analysis of smart specialisation strategies both at theoretical and practical levels. It has been written at a critical period in the implementation of smart specialisation strategies in every region in Europe. The fact that the EU has adopted smart specialisation as a mandatory principle for every region and member state will make this book useful to policy makers, analysts and researchers.

Dominique Foray is Full Professor of Economics and Management of Innovation at the École polytechnique fédérale de Lausanne (EPFL), Switzerland.

D1678214

Regions and Cities

Series Editor in Chief
Susan M. Christopherson, *Cornell University, USA*

Editors
Maryann Feldman, *University of Georgia, USA*
Gernot Grabher, *HafenCity University Hamburg, Germany*
Ron Martin, *University of Cambridge, UK*
Martin Perry, *Massey University, New Zealand*

In today's globalised, knowledge-driven and networked world, regions and cities have assumed heightened significance as the interconnected nodes of economic, social and cultural production, and as sites of new modes of economic and territorial governance and policy experimentation. This book series brings together incisive and critically engaged international and interdisciplinary research on this resurgence of regions and cities, and should be of interest to geographers, economists, sociologists, political scientists and cultural scholars, as well as to policy-makers involved in regional and urban development.

For more information on the Regional Studies Association visit www.regionalstudies.org

There is a **30% discount** available to RSA members on books in the *Regions and Cities* series, and other subject related Taylor and Francis books and e-books including Routledge titles. To order just e-mail alex.robinson@tandf.co.uk, or phone on +44 (0) 20 7017 6924 and declare your RSA membership. You can also visit www.routledge.com and use the discount code: **RSA0901**

Smart Specialisation
Opportunities and challenges for regional innovation policy

Dominique Foray

 Routledge
Taylor & Francis Group

LONDON AND NEW YORK

First published 2015
by Routledge
2 Park Square, Milton Park, Abingdon, Oxfordshire OX14 4RN

and by Routledge
711 Third Avenue, New York, NY 10017

First issued in paperback 2015

Routledge is an imprint of the Taylor & Francis Group, an informa business

British Library Cataloguing in Publication Data
A catalogue record for this book is available from the British Library.

Library of Congress Cataloging in Publication Data
Foray, Dominique.
 Smart specialisation : opportunities and challenges for regional innovation policy / Dominique Foray.
  pages cm
 Includes bibliographical references and index.
 1. Technological innovation–Government policy. 2. Regional economics.
3. Regional planning. 4. Sustainable development. I. Title.
  HC79.T4F647 2014
  338.9–dc23
                    2014006113

ISBN 13: 978-1-138-92365-2 (pbk)
ISBN 13: 978-1-13877-672-2 (hbk)

Typeset in Times New Roman
by Taylor & Francis Books

Contents

Illustrations

Figures

Boxes

Acknowledgements

The extraordinary adventure of smart specialisation strategy within the context of European regional policies gave me the opportunity to meet many people and participate in numerous collaborations. Some of these encounters were expected, while others were pleasant surprises!

I'm thinking first of all of the *Knowledge for Growth* Expert Group, within which the concept was created (Chapter 1), and especially Paul David, Bronwyn Hall and Bart van Ark, who co-authored the first two short papers on this subject with me. I would also like to thank Manuel Trajtenberg, who wrote the foreword, and J. C. Caldeira, K. Debaekere, K. Frenken, T. Giannitsis, L. Tsipouri, D. Guellec, D. Harhoff, G. Licht, J. Mairesse, R. Marimon, N. Phelps, L. Soete, P. Stephan, E. Steinmueller, R. Veugelers and X. Vence, who provided many useful comments and ideas at different times during this adventure.

In mentioning the Expert Group, I must pay tribute to the Commissioner himself – J. Potočnik – whose unwavering interest in our work and regular participation in our meetings undoubtedly stimulated the efforts of our group. I also wish to mention the permanent officials of the European Commission, whose dynamism and competence I appreciated. There are many but I would particularly like to thank X. Goenega (who played two determining roles as administrator of the Expert Group at DG RESEARCH and Director of the RIS3 Platform) and M. Landabaso at DG REGIO, as well as their respective teams in Seville, Spain, and Brussels, Belgium.

I also had the pleasure of collaborating with an academic community that I was unfamiliar with and with which I had a particularly rewarding dialogue and exchange. I am thinking particularly of P. McCann, thanks to whom I learned a great deal, as well as J. Goddard, K. Morgan, M. Navarro and R. Ortega-Argilés, all experts in the domains of regional innovation systems and regional policies. The most enjoyable and also the most surprising encounters occurred in the regional agencies and administrations, where I worked with these 'local heroes' who play such an important role, as mentioned in Chapter 5, and without whom nothing would have been possible. I'm thinking especially of J. Larosse (Flanders), F. Pinna (Centre), D. Dareys (Aquitaine), S. Anquetil (Alsace), A. Torelli (Marche), W. Reek (Friesland), V. Gongolidis (Greece) and many others. My thanks to you all!

Although my research group – the Chair of Economics and Management of Innovation (at the College of Management, EPFL) did not fundamentally participate in my work on smart specialisation, I cannot leave unacknowledged the important place occupied by my PhD and postdoctoral students, both past and present, in my research activities. I would like to express my gratitude for their energy, their talent and their curiosity. Special thanks go to Anna-Maria Conti, Patrick Gaulé, Intan Hamdan-Livramento, Marcel Bogers, Marianna Marino, Markus Simeth, Stefano Barrufaldi, Viviana Munoz Tellez, Monica Coffano, Claudia Pellegrin, Julio Raffo, Fabiana Visentin and Michele Pezzoni.

Last but not least, I would like to thank Cyrielle Blanc for her great administrative and organisational support, Margaret Howett for her excellent translation and editing work and Patrick Bays for creating the figures.

Lausanne, 31 January 2014

Abbreviations

DG REGIO	Directorate-General for Regional and Urban Policy
DG RESEARCH	Directorate-General for Research and Innovation
EC	European Commission
ERDF	European Regional Development Fund
EU	European Union
GPT	General Purpose Technologies and Tools
GVC	Global Value Chain
ICT	Information and Communications Technology
INRA	French National Institute for Agricultural Research
IPTS	Institute for Prospective and Technological Studies
IT	Information Technology
JRC	Joint Research Centre
KEEN	Knowledge and Excellence in European Nanotechnology
KETS	Key Enabling Technologies
OECD	Organisation of Economic Co-operation and Development
PRO	Public Research Organisation
R&D	Research and Development
R&I	Research and Innovation
RIS3	Research and Innovation Strategies for Smart Specialisation
RTDI	Research, Technological Development and Innovation
SME	Small and Medium-sized Enterprise
S3P	Smart Specialisation Platform
UAV	Unmanned Aerial Vehicle
VC	Venture Capital Organisation

Foreword

Smart Specialization: a smart new policy paradigm for challenging times

Manuel Trajtenberg[1]

As typically happens in other realms, policy paradigms and consequent pre-scriptions tend to experience 'diminishing returns', that is, their usefulness declines the more they are applied, and as time goes by they may become irrelevant altogether. R&D and innovation policies, and more generally 'industrial policies', have undergone several transformations in the past few decades, including protectionist policies under the conceptual umbrella of 'infant industries', outright picking winners (e.g. VLSI in Japan), supporting R&D investments through tax advantages or grants, SMEs' preferential treatment, regional devel-opment schemes, and so forth. There has been a large variance in the precise formulation of these policies and, if only because of the observed variety, the verdict is still out in terms of how well these various strategies have played out in fostering sustained growth. However, several useful lessons have been learned, among them:

1   Do not attempt to 'pick winners' – governments cannot know better than the market, and certainly not more than its quintessential driving force, the entrepreneurs;
2   Favour as much as possible 'neutral' policy instruments, i.e. those that have a generic make-up and hence do not discriminate a priori among activities, industries or players;
3   Be humble in designing policy, i.e. recognize that the economic and technolo-gical reality evolves faster than we can grasp at any point in time, and therefore policies should always have a strong learning and evolutionary component;
4   Endow policies with a 'self-destruct' mechanism so that they can be easily terminated as soon as strong diminishing returns (or worse) settle in;
5   Factor in global forces – every aspiring nation wants to have its 'Silicon Valley' and its MIT. Indeed, there are now many more potential compe-titors, so do not even try to swim against the (global) current, nor to protect for long your upcoming contenders from the pack of relentless, speedy and ruthless rivals that await them around the corner.

Tough precepts to follow. Is the result an empty policy set? Not quite, but sharp conceptualization skills as much as profound empirical knowledge are needed in order to formulate policy strategies that would be both relevant for the challenging realities of post-crisis Europe, and compliant with these precepts. Dominique Foray, together with his co-authors, brings both attributes to bear in drafting and crafting 'Smart Specialization' as a new policy paradigm. The key to its appeal lies in the delicate balance it strikes, on the one hand, between the understanding that there is no substitute for naturally arising entrepreneurship and local comparative advantages and, on the other hand, the realization that for any policy-relevant horizon, chances are that many (most?) potentially potent innovational developments may not happen for lack of any number of complementary factors. Thus, there is ample justification and wide scope for policy prescriptions aimed at triggering and supporting activities that could fill the missing parts. In so doing such policies may appear to deviate from neutrality in the narrow sense, but not in intent and focus.

No wonder that Smart Specialization has become so fast a favourite among policy circles in Europe and beyond. It incorporates the distilled insights from decades of economic research and policy experimentation. I commend Professor Dominique Foray for making this book available to the wide community of economic scholars and policy-makers, which is surely going to foster the development of ever more refined policy ideas along the lines of Smart Specialization. It is nice to witness (smart) economics reclaiming its relevance in post-crisis Europe.

Tel Aviv, 30 January 2014

Note

1 Manuel Trajtenberg is Professor at the Eitan Berglas School of Economics, Tel Aviv University, Israel; Research Associate at The National Bureau of Economic Research; and Chairman of the Planning and Budgeting Committee of Higher Education.

Introduction

The notion of *smart specialisation* describes the capacity of an economic system (a region for example) to generate new specialities through the discovery of new domains of opportunity and the local concentration and agglomeration of resources and competences in these domains. Such a capacity is needed to initiate structural changes in the form of diversification, transition, modernisation or the radical foundation of industries and/or services.

Tourism in any alpine region is not a *smart* specialisation just because this sector is important economically in this region. However, the development of new information and communications technology (ICT) applications aimed at significantly changing the operational processes of tourism services or enriching the tourism supply can become a smart specialisation if the new activity attracts enough efforts and resources, and drives the construction of new competitive advantages at the intersection between the tourism sector and ICT as a generic technology.

Fisheries and the canning industry in Galicia, Spain, are again not a *smart* specialisation, even if this sector is economically important in this region. However, the creation of a university in Vigo (*Campus do Mar*) to develop applied science and technological solutions to improve the operational efficiency of traditional fisheries can drive some kind of smart specialisation if a population of firms specialising in the development of these solutions emerges and grows from the merging of the traditional sector and certain applied science domains (bioengineering, chemical engineering, ICT).

Again, textile and silk industries cannot be viewed as a *smart* specialisation in the Lyon region (France) during the twentieth century just because they constituted an important sector. However, the activity of integrating polymers and other composite materials into production processes was likely to trigger a strong transition of certain segments of the silk industry towards technical materials, thereby giving rise to a successful smart specialisation.

The notion of smart specialisation defines a worthy process of diversification through the local concentration of resources and competences in a certain number of new domains that represent possible paths for the transformation of productive structures. As these three examples show, a smart specialisation process is embedded in productive structures and capacities that are local but whose transformation requires new resources, new technologies and new competences, perhaps generated within the same local area although they may also come from outside. In each example, what can emerge as a smart specialisation is a new activity where an innovative project *complements* existing productive assets. Firms form the centre of gravity – the kingpin – of such processes because they are in the best position to explore and test new avenues of innovation and structural changes, in collaboration with research structures and other social organisations.

Turning now to the notion of smart specialisation *strategy*, this involves putting in place a process whereby such a dynamic of new speciality development, related to existing production structures, can be facilitated thanks to punctual and targeted governmental intervention in order to support in a *preferential* way the most promising new activities in terms of discovery, experimentation, potential spillover and structural changes.

The two notions – smart specialisation and smart specialisation strategies – should not be confused. History is brimming with successful smart specialisation processes that occurred spontaneously, without any policy, thanks to the discovery and coordination capacities of the private agents themselves. I will describe below some cases of smart specialisation without policy. This is an ideal situation that is of course unlikely to happen for many reasons; hence, the necessity for policy and strategies when regional systems are suffering from collective myopia or inertia or more simply need to start afresh.

1 Smart specialisation strategy and policy

Setting up such a process in every European region has become an important objective of European Union (EU) Cohesion Policy – known as RIS3 (*Research and Innovation Strategies for Smart Specialisation*). In the next chapter, I will briefly explore the academic origins of the concept and then its transposition into the domain of regional innovation policies. The basic idea governing the generalised adoption of smart specialisation strategy within the framework of Cohesion Policy was to effect a change of paradigm in the way in which these regional innovation policies were structured; the goal is now to encourage each region to identify transformation priorities that reflect and amplify existing local structures and competences, and thus produce original and unique competitive advantages. As one of the advocates of smart specialisation policy initially argued (David, 2010):

> such strategies have a chance to yield results that will be superior to the past tendencies produced by undifferentiated (EC or OECD or World Bank) recommendations for undifferentiated 'best policy practices' – encouraging countries and in turn local government authorities all to set their sights on doing the same 'good things' to foster the same forms of innovation.

Policy design

With regard to the implementation of this process, I think that it is particularly important to follow certain design principles in order that the policy process preserves and respects the virtues of the decentralised entrepreneurial dynamic, while allowing the region and its principal actors to realise their vision concerning the future positioning of the region in the knowledge economy.

This policy design focuses particularly on:

- The importance of *the entrepreneurial discovery* as the principal source of information regarding the new exploration and transformation activities that are likely to be prioritised. Administration and politics no longer play the role of omniscient planner but are prepared to listen to entrepreneurs, researchers and citizens in order to identify priorities and facilitate the emergence and growth of new activities.[1]
- The *level of granularity* at which projects are detected (or possibly constructed) and priorities are established. Neither the sector nor the individual level is relevant. Preference will be given to a mid-grained level of aggregation – the level at which activities group together a certain number of firms and partners that collectively explore and discover a new pathway to transformation.
- The *inclusive nature* of the strategy, which implies not that all sectors and all territories are represented in the strategy but that each sector and each territory has a chance to be included in it thanks to the shaping of attractive and promising structural transformation projects. Thanks to this strategy, the frontier between traditional sectors and the so-called 'modern' sectors of the regional economy is no longer rigid since the particularity of an inclusive strategy is precisely to shift certain traditional segments over to the modern part of the economy.
- The fact is that today's new activities will no longer be new tomorrow and they will therefore be replaced by new 'new activities'. By definition, the strategy is *progressive* and always aims to seize new opportunities and new options for transformation that appear over time.
- The *experimental nature* of this policy: perhaps certain experiments will fail. To reduce the cost of these possible failures, a coherent, rigorous and transparent set of indicators and metrics must be put in place.

A smart specialisation policy emphasises the principle of prioritisation in a *non-neutral* manner (to favour certain technologies, fields, populations of firms) and defines a method to identify such desirable areas for innovation policy intervention.[2] The main goal of a smart specialisation policy is to concentrate resources on the development of *those activities that are likely to effectively transform the existing economic structures through R&D and innovation*. Such activities, if they meet a certain number of criteria (see Box 3.2), should represent the locus for resource concentration and prioritisation.

Why prioritisation and resource concentration are important?

Significant returns to size and critical mass in R&D and other innovation-related activities are empirically identified in numerous academic papers. These activities have scale and agglomeration economies (Henderson and Cockburn, 1996; Agrawal, Cockburn and Oettl, 2010; Agrawal and Cockburn, 2003; Trajtenberg, 2002). Although based on different methods and illustrating various dimensions of inventive and innovative activities, all this empirical evidence says the same thing: there are substantial indivisibilities in knowledge production at both micro and macro levels. Gains from specialisation are central in R&D; even the ability to capture knowledge spillovers generated by others depends on the existence of a sufficiently large R&D sector in close proximity. Small is not necessarily more beautiful in the information age. *The logic of economies of scale, economies of scope and spillovers, as essential determinants of the productivity of R&D and other innovation-related activities is intact.*

If you are small, you are not in a good position to generate critical mass in R&D in all sectors so you have to be smarter. Concentrating resources in a few domains and focusing efforts will generate size and critical mass effects that would not occur if you do a little of everything.

Thus, a preferential policy may be needed to concentrate resources locally and strengthen a small number of new activities so that a growth process through agglomeration and entries can happen. These new activities – if they have been selected intelligently – will have many positive effects:

- Improving the performance of the sectors concerned.
- Building capabilities and expanding the knowledge base towards new domains of R&D and innovation.
- Generating spillovers to the *connected* domains of the regional economy.

Particularisation

However, the idea of focusing on a particular domain is not enough to define a smart specialisation strategy. The focusing process should aim to develop distinctive and fertile areas of specialisation for the future. Strongly mimetic regional programmes to promote export-capacity expansion in certain fashionable high-tech domains or to foster industrial agglomerations of high-tech firms that duplicate the efforts of neighbouring states or provinces have the effect in the EU setting of dissipating potential gains from agglomeration economies. They also vitiate efforts to create multiple lines of regional and national specialisation that are sustainably profitable.[3] In such cases, regions compete for the same resources, with none making any significant impact.

In short, regions should practise resource concentration and focus by developing distinctive and original areas of specialisation. 'They need to particularise themselves.'[4]

Why entrepreneurial discovery is important?

This principle is so important that any smart specialisation policy 'model' that did not include this provision would have an entirely different character. Why is it so important? Prioritising certain technologies or domains always entails an element of risk because this implies predicting the future development of technologies and markets. Horizontal policies might be difficult to achieve but the likelihood of being wrong is minimised; i.e. the identification of *what to do* is not so difficult: everybody knows about the direct and indirect framework conditions that foster innovation (see Aghion, 2006). In contrast, the identification of *desirable areas of intervention* in a more vertical fashion (what technology? what sub-systems?) is extremely difficult and entails great risk.

Discovering the right domains for future specialisation in the knowledge economy is no trivial matter, especially when we abandon the representation of the omniscient central planner who knows beforehand what should be done: the government does not have innate wisdom or *ex-ante* knowledge about future priorities. We must guard against the intellectual logic imposed by the 'principal-agent model', according to which the principal (the government) knows from the start which specialities should be developed, and therefore confines itself to establishing incentives for private industry to implement the plan (Rodrik, 2013b). 'What if, as I and many others assume, there are no principals ... with the robust and panoramic knowledge needed for this directive role?' (Sabel, 2004: p. 3).

Furthermore, technology foresight exercises or critical technology surveys mandated by regional or national administrations tend to produce the same ranking of priorities without any consideration for the context and specific conditions of the client for whom the exercise is undertaken. Too many regions have selected the same technology mix – a little of everything – showing a lack of imagination, creativity and strategic vision.

Therefore, the discovery process – discovering which domains of R&D and innovative activities a region should move into to build its future in the knowledge economy – is an issue in its own right. Thus, the discovery and collective-experimentation process forms an integral part of political action and must be carried out within the framework of strategic interactions between the government and the private sector. This is the essence of entrepreneurial discovery.

If accomplished properly through an entrepreneurial discovery process, the smart specialisation strategy should logically identify not necessarily the hottest domain in nanotechnology/biotechnology/ICTs, but rather the domains where new R&D and innovation activities will complement the region's other productive assets to create future domestic and interregional competitive advantages. Simply put, a successful strategy will not be found by reading the tables of contents of the most recent issues of *Science* or *Nature*, but rather by observing the structures of the economy and supporting the discovery processes undertaken by firms and other operators in this economy.

Combining two approaches to political action

The novelty of such a policy is that, while addressing the issue of supporting the development of new specialities and activities through *preferential* interventions, it will try to promote and support the decentralised decisions of entrepreneurs concerning R&D, innovation and structural changes. In other words, this policy is an attempt to reconcile two approaches to political action that are usually considered to be in potential conflict:

- The first approach involves setting priorities – not *horizontal* priorities such as improving human capital, developing good universities or building an effective intellectual property rights system – but *vertical* ones regarding particular fields and technologies as well as particular sets or networks of actors.
- The second approach is less controversial. It involves decentralised entrepreneurial initiatives and competitive entries – in other words, the set of factors now recognised as the true engine for innovation and economic growth (Baumol, 2002; Phelps, 2013).

The only way to reconcile these two ideas is for policy-makers seeking vertical priorities to rely on an *entrepreneurial discovery process*. In other words, the search for, and identification of, priorities will be carried out from the grass-roots level, not just from the top.

In suggesting these policy design principles, particularly that of entrepreneurial discovery, the European Commission (EC) has opted to establish a process in each region that will enable them to generate new evolution dynamics by opening up new domains of opportunity, without any danger of homogenising the system or hampering existing structures. On the contrary, what must be established is a decentralised dynamic process that should ensure the continuous transformation of productive structures through research and innovation, a transformation that goes far beyond the high-tech domain and concerns the entire regional economy.

2 A note on the meaning of specialisation

The notion of specialisation used in this framework is certainly specific. The meaning of specialisation as employed in the smart specialisation framework does not refer to the usual indicator of the share of an industry in a region divided by the share of that industry in the whole country. In such cases, specialisation is expressed in relative terms and measuring it does not provide any information about localisation (agglomeration) economies and does not measure regional concentration. This is why the fact that a region has some smart specialisations should not be understood as indicating that it is specialised relative to other regions in a passive sense, but rather *it has developed new specialities based on regional concentration of knowledge and competences.*

It follows from this discussion that most of the indicators used hitherto have not really reached the right target, namely measuring smart specialisation. Rather, they provide measures of relative (scientific and technological) specialisations of regions and countries. This is, of course, a useful way of characterising scientific and technological profiles of regional or national economies but this approach fails to characterise and measure the concentration of activities, knowledge and competences that give rise to positive locational effects. This is why the research agenda for developing a framework of indicators to measure entrepreneurial discovery and smart specialisation is as yet by no means complete.

3 The wonderful and rapid career of a policy idea

This policy concept has enjoyed a short but exciting life. Elaborated by a group of innovation scholars in 2008 and 2009, it quickly made a significant impact on the policy audience, particularly in Europe. The concept is now a key element of the EU 2020 Innovation Union initiative[5] – the Commission has decided to build a platform of services (RIS3 platform) to support regions in their efforts to devise and implement a smart specialisation strategy.[6] Moreover, in Annex IV of the draft structural funds regulations, smart specialisation is set as a conditionality for two thematic objectives of the future Cohesion Policy (R&I target and ICT target).[7] Last but not least, the Organisation for Economic Co-Operation and Develppment (OECD) (2012) as well as the World Bank are launching activities for promoting smart specialisation in other parts of the world.

The passage from conceptualisation to the general implementation of the policy in the EU has perhaps been too short and policy-makers would probably have been better off proceeding first to *clinical trials* and pilot experiments before applying the treatment to the whole population of regions. At present, trials are not mandatory in policy research and there is no federal administration to examine the trial results and give or refuse the regulatory authorisation. However, it is too late to lament this; the short-track option was chosen by the EU and it is time to remind ourselves of the purpose of this exercise, or at least the purpose intended by the initial authors. What are the opportunities and stakes for each region concerned and how can this policy be implemented to respect its spirit, while adapting its practical application to the local conditions and historical circumstances that make each region an individual case?

4 The book

In this book I will examine first the origin of the concept of smart specialisation and identify the basic shared arguments and facts that have made it possible for smart specialisation to have 'political salience' and make policy-makers eager to 'do it'. In Chapter 2 the dynamics of smart specialisation are presented and documented with many examples and the case for a smart specialisation policy (or strategy) is made. A smart specialisation policy is characterised in terms of a particular process of resource allocation (vertical) and the policy design challenge is presented and discussed, including how to make a non-neutral policy aimed at concentrating resources in a vertical fashion compatible with decentralised and entrepreneurial innovation activities. In Chapter 3 the principles and methods of smart specialisation policy are described and explained and particular attention is paid to the concept of entrepreneurial discovery, which is the key solution to the policy design problem raised above. In Chapter 4 the goals of smart specialisation are differentiated according to regional development and other contextual factors. Finally, Chapter 5 is about practical implementation issues, as well as addressing the question of political and policy capabilities of regional administrations.

This book might be deemed 'strange' at first glance since it cannot yet report on any evidence to assess the efficiency of this policy, a task that will be necessary and feasible at the end of the next EU budgetary period – i.e. after a certain period of time has elapsed since the launch of the strategy. However, this policy already exists in practice. All European regions are in the process of building and implementing a smart specialisation strategy and more than 153 regions as well as 15 countries are currently registered on the Smart Specialisation Platform (S3P) in Seville to exchange and interact about their smart specialisation strategies.[8] This is why it is certainly necessary to provide a synthesis of the views and intellectual projects that were shared by the initial authors. What are the main principles that were formulated as the building blocks of the policy process and for what kind of goals? What sort of potential benefits are expected from the wide adoption of this policy both at regional and European levels? What are the main challenges and potential risks that can arise from misunderstandings and bad implementation? It is also interesting to propose an initial synthesis of the way in which regions have 'absorbed' the strategy and started to give an operational content to its main concepts. Thus, my book aims to articulate a coherent vision of the policy approach that is evoked by the term *smart specialisation strategy*, and to explore and elaborate the requirements and implications that are consistent with giving operational content to that conceptualisation.

The growing popularity of smart specialisation in diverse circles, as well as the fact that its initial formulation left considerable latitude for policy-makers to interpret the specific content and implications of its prescriptions in any particular set of circumstances, have generated a plethora of ideas as to what 'smart specialisation' means for economic development and growth policies. In my view, smart specialisation strategy is not just a new term to describe 'a good regional innovation policy'. It entails a different process of resource allocation that creates both *opportunities* for policy-makers and stakeholders to transform structures and *challenges* in terms of policy design, processes and institutions. Although, there are certainly other conceptual frameworks and corresponding policy priorities that would also merit consideration, I remain convinced that interpretation of the smart specialisation that has recently shaped European regional innovation policies will emerge as an especially fruitful source of empirically and theoretically grounded economic policy insights – for Europe and other regions of the world.

Notes

1 There is a large strand of literature devoted to the concept of 'entrepreneurial discovery' in the Austrian Economics school of thought (Kirzner, 1997). However, our use of this concept is inspired more by its pragmatic application in Development Economics. More specifically, the notion of entrepreneurial discovery used in the smart specialisation framework draws on works in development economics and new industrial policy, in particular R. Hausman and D. Rodrik's view of development as 'a self-discovery process'. See Hausmann and Rodrik (2003).

2 A non-neutral policy is one that selects projects according to preferred fields, sectors or technologies, while a neutral policy only responds to demands arising spontaneously from industry activity (definition taken from Trajtenberg, 2002).

3 For analytical development of this argument, see P.A. David, 1984, 1999.

4 Oral communication, P.A. David, *Knowledge for Growth* meeting. For more information on the *Knowledge for Growth* Expert Group, see Chapter 1.

5 See *Europe 2020 Flagship Initiative Innovation Union*, Communication from the Commission to the European Parliament, the Council, the European Economic and Social Committee and the Committee of the Regions, European Commission, COM (2010).

6 http://s3platform.jrc.eu.europa.eu.

7 See *Regional Policy Contributing to Smart Growth in Europe 2020*, Communication from the Commission to the European Parliament, the Council, the European Economic and Social Committee and the Committee of the Regions, SEC (2010) 1183 and *Fact Sheet: Research Innovation Strategies for Smart Specialisation*, DG REGIO, European Commission, 2011.

8 These were the figures as at June 2014.

1   The origin

The notion of smart specialisation was conceived around 2009, in a very specific place, the *Knowledge for Growth* Expert Group, composed of growth and innovation economists. It must be emphasised, however, that the analysis of the spatial, and especially regional, dimensions of innovation policies – whose development lies at the crossroads between geographical economics and technological change economics – was conceived well before that and was already widespread both within the academic community and in the public-policy arena.

It is therefore logical that the smart specialisation concept very quickly attracted the interest of regional development policy specialists.

1 *Knowledge for growth* (2005–09)

The origins of the idea are to be found in the discussions and communications that animated the *Knowledge for Growth* Expert Group established by Research Commissioner J. Potočnik in 2005.[1] These origins are strongly connected to discussions within the group about foreign R&D in European regions and the ways in which these regions could be more attractive to global firms' location strategies (Foray and van Ark, 2008). One main conceptual argument in the discussion was that the logic of territorial attractiveness is based on the scarcity of a specific resource: the economies of agglomeration themselves (David, 1999). This rare resource is depleted by the proliferation of sites competing to capture the same assets. The related argument was that this is an accurate description of the European situation because of the combined effects of two factors.

First, the public research system in Europe remains fragmented and nationally based, limiting agglomeration processes and hampering the formation of world-class centres. This fragmentation has limited the natural development of the hubs whose growth should unrestrictedly be nurtured to support the expansion of the knowledge economy. With certain rare exceptions, agglomeration processes associated with public research operate within national systems and resource flows do not cross borders.

Second, we observe a definite tendency in Europe for countries and regions to do the same thing and envisage their future in a similar fashion. Every European region prides itself on having an investment plan in information and communications technology (ICT), biotechnology and nanotechnology. In most regions, decision-makers have defined priorities without any evidence of their prospects for success.

National-level fragmentation of public research systems and the duplication of knowledge bases have contributed to a collection of sub-critical systems in Europe, all doing more or less the same thing, systems that are unattractive entrants in the world localisation tournament. Such a situation is obviously a source of inefficiency. Economies of scale and spillover potentials are not fully realised and the potential economies of agglomeration are dissipated, resulting in a system composed of too many unappealing sites. Imitative and duplicative policies aimed at creating the next 'miracle growth' region, capturing a leading position in a major segment of headline industries such as semiconductors, biotechnology, automobiles or mass-market software, not only create slender chances for any region to succeed, they also perpetuate patterns of market dominance with leaders and followers.

This was the starting point of the analysis from which emerged the idea that one possible solution for those regions under threat from the locational tournament and global competition involves building aptitudes to *particularise themselves* by generating and stimulating the growth of new exploration and research activities, which are related to existing productive structures and show the potential to transform those structures. This is the rationale for *smart specialisation* (Foray *et al.* 2009, 2011).

Thus, from the start, the idea of a smart specialisation policy was not conceived as a planning doctrine that would require a region to specialise in a particular set of industries. Instead, it seeks robust and transparent means for nominating those activities, at regional level, that seem likely to benefit from R&D and innovation. Therefore, rather than offering a method for determining whether a hypothetical region has a 'strength' in a particular set of activities, a smart specialisation strategy emphasises the formation of capabilities and the design of institutions to support entrepreneurial discovery and the early growth of the most promising activities that have been discovered. Rather than suggesting, for instance, that Galicia, Spain, which has an important fisheries sector, should intensify its specialisation in this industry, smart specialisation policy provides a means to assess whether fisheries would benefit from more R&D and innovation and whether Galicia should 'specialise' in the development of new innovative solutions for this industry.

This also means that a smart specialisation strategy must address the missing connections that should be made between R&D and innovation activities, on the one hand, and the sectoral structure of the economy, on the other.

2 From academic idea to *ex ante* conditionality

At a time of economic crisis and public finance failures, the main concerns and solutions of national governments and European Union (EU) administrations have focused on macroeconomic stability and the dramatic reduction of public deficits. While this is probably a necessary answer, it has totally failed – for obvious reasons – in mobilising European society towards gratifying or even exhilarating objectives (Ahner and Landabaso, 2011; Landabaso, 2014). What smart specialisation strategy provides precisely is a framework and a means for regional administrations and regional stakeholders to take things in hand again. It allows them to organise collective efforts in order to formulate a credible innovation strategy, thereby providing a positive response to the problems of regions that are a medium- and long-term threat to growth and employment. The smart specialisation framework encourages policy-makers and stakeholders to ask themselves the important questions about the future of their region: where do we want to see our region positioning itself in the future knowledge economy and how do we implement the policies necessary to conform to our collective and strategic vision?

The political salience of smart specialisation strategies

Thinking more precisely about what has made it possible for smart specialisation to have 'political salience' and made policy-makers eager to 'do it', I would mention the following four points:

- First, by encouraging regions to reflect on their future in the knowledge economy. What are the activities that we wish to develop and what structural changes do we wish to make? The exercise has in a way served as catalyst for collective deliberation that has mobilised and often stimulated regional actors of innovation.
- Second, the principles of entrepreneurial discovery and inclusive strategy (see Chapter 2 and Chapter 3), even if they have often seemed abstract and academic, have served to show that this policy is not merely a purely technocratic exercise, nor solely a policy concentrated on high-tech innovation, but an open and complete strategy.
- Third, the smart specialisation framework is particularly concerned with regions that are less advanced. It is not a strategy reserved for the best. On the contrary, it is likely to represent a unique way for less advanced regions to dramatically improve their capabilities in certain domains.
- Finally, implementing a smart specialisation strategy was not only viewed as 'locally' desirable, but was also regarded as a means of achieving greater efficiency in resource allocation and coordination of activities at system level (member-state and EU level).

I will discuss these properties of smart specialisation in several different parts of this book.

EU processes and decisions: when smart specialisation meets the development of a 'different regional innovation policy'

As part of the Europe 2020 strategy, the EC adopted the Innovation Union flagship initiative in October 2010.[2] This initiative provides a framework within which a comprehensive innovation strategy can be established for Europe to enhance its capacity to deliver smart, sustainable and inclusive growth. The initiative also generated strong policy guidance to influence the design of regional research and innovation strategies in order to maximise the efficiency of the allocation of public resources. This is where the principle of smart specialisation emerged as a strategic and integrated approach at regional level. The principle was designed to be instrumental in investing Structural Funds more efficiently in the areas of two key objectives: strengthening research, technological development and innovation (R&I target); and enhancing access to and use of information and communication technologies (ICT target).[3]

Smart specialisation is one of the 10 features for well-performing national and regional research and innovation systems, according to the Innovation Union's self-assessment tool. More importantly, it is a key element of the European Commission's proposal for a reformed Cohesion Policy as *ex ante* conditionality for use of the European Regional Development Fund (ERDF) during the next Structural Funds programming period 2014–20. This means it is a pre-condition related to the effective use of EU funds, which should be fulfilled by the time an Operational Programme is approved.

To help the regions prepare their smart specialisation strategy, the Commission has developed quite a large infrastructure – in particular the Research and Innovation Strategies for Smart Specialisation (RIS3) Platform hosted by the Joint Research Centre (JRC) Institute for Prospective Technological Studies (IPTS) in Seville, Spain, that provides technical assistance and develops a programme of peer reviews, knowledge sharing and experience exchanges.[4] This platform grew rapidly between 2011 and 2013 as the information and knowledge needs of the regions increased considerably.

Development of new regional policies as the crucible of smart specialisation strategies

While the intellectual origin of the idea was the *Knowledge for Growth* Expert Group created by the Directorate-General for Research, it was the Directorate-General for Regional and Urban Policy (DG REGIO), led by EU Commissioner J. Hahn, that played a central role in the next developments – including the instrumentalisation of smart specialisation as *ex-ante* conditionality, as well as the implementation of this strategy in every region in Europe between 2011 and 2013. For the DG REGIO, it is the result of several decades of reinforcing its regional policies promoting research and innovation. The European Commission's first regional innovation policies were launched in 1993–94. Then the approach became widespread: 33 regional strategies were under development between 1996 and 1999 (European Commission, 2002). These policies were essentially horizontal, concentrating on the framework conditions favourable to innovation in SMEs. As from the turn of the century however, certain experts observed that the way in which Structural Funds were used to support innovation was not very effective: 'Based on physical infrastructure improvement, direct grants to firms and foreign investment attraction, traditional regional policy has not proved very successful in promoting innovation, in particular in less-favoured regions in the European Union' (Landabaso and Mouton, 2005: p. 209). Based on this assessment, *different* regional innovation strategies were gradually envisaged; in other words, strategies aimed at establishing regional innovation *systems* (Landabaso and Mouton, 2005: p. 235; Landabaso, 1997; Landabaso and Reid, 1999). This approach was favoured during the period 2000–06, during which 135 regions (out of 156) adopted this policy of establishing a regional innovation system on the basis of finance provided by the European Regional Development Fund (ERDF). This intellectual development occurring within the DG REGIO was marked particularly by the actions of Commissioner D. Hübner; it culminated in the publication of the Barca report (2009), resulted in the concept of *place-based innovation strategies* (Barca *et al.* 2012; McCann and Ortega-Argilés, 2013a) and created the intellectual conditions favouring acceptability of the smart specialisation strategy approach as a new stage in the regional innovation policy structuring effort within the EU.[5]

Cluster policy as forerunner?

Parallel to the deployment of regional innovation strategies, a wave of cluster policies swept across Europe and elsewhere, imposing a certain public intervention model in favour of the constitution of technological clusters and critical mass, inspired by the works of M. Porter (1998) and wonderful stories emanating from California. The aim of these policies is to encourage the spatial agglomeration of a given activity with a view to gaining certain benefits from this agglomeration.[6] A multitude of clusters therefore appeared all over Europe,[7] but more as the result of voluntarist public policies without always reflecting a real economic and entrepreneurial dynamic. The key here is not to deny the importance for innovation of positive local knowledge externalities – widely observed and measured in the empirical literature[8] – but rather to observe that the latter cannot in themselves justify a cluster policy (Chatterji *et al.* 2013). Furthermore, the economic fundamentals of the activity in question must also be solid. Therefore the economic literature recognises few justifications for cluster policies (arguing notably that it is an extremely difficult policy to implement with regard to the coordination problems to be resolved, and that the benefits gained are usually minimal – see

Duranton, 2011; Aghion *et al.*, 2009). They are also approaches that are likely to hamper existing structures instead of stimulating their transformation and diversification. Thus, they are approaches that often amount to endlessly financing application-oriented research activities, without these applications ever being transformed into innovation and economic knowledge.

As underlined by Feldman and Francis (2001), the story of *cluster* policies is often the story of a certain fascination for a phenomenon that we wish to imitate but whose basis we do not understand:

> Looking at a successful region in its full maturity may not provide pre-scriptive information about how such regions do develop. Conditions that we associate with an entrepreneurial environment are the result of a functioning entrepreneurship and do not illuminate the early efforts by which such entrepreneurship first took hold and the cluster developed.

Smart specialisation strategies thus constitute as much a continuity of as a break with cluster policy practices: continuity, of course, as local resource concentration is a major objective of smart specialisation strategies; break too, however, as smart specialisation strategy focuses on *the early effort*, the opening of a domain and the emergence of a new activity, as the preliminary and fundamental phase of any clustering process. It puts regional innovation strategy back on its feet, so to speak, by attributing greater importance to entrepreneurial discovery: namely, the establishment and collective exploration of new areas of opportunity, which will possibly form the basis for the local resource concentration and increasing returns associated with clustering effects.

Concerns, doubts

There were, however, serious doubts about the viability of a smart specialisation strategy for *any* region. Of course, it would be marvellous if every region could develop a sound, knowledge-driven strategy to build competitive advantages through R&D and innovation in specific domains, but are there enough technologies to provide opportunities to all regions? Are there enough 'roles' in the knowledge economy 'play'? Is there a risk that some regions will not get a share of the knowledge economy, even if they would like to have a smart specialisation strategy? I think that numerous opportunities exist if the smart specialisation strategy is set at the right level of granularity, at the sub-system rather than the sectoral level, as will be argued in Chapter 3.

Also, the very word 'specialisation' is prone to misunderstanding and mis-interpretation. As already pointed out, smart specialisation does not aim to rehabilitate a philosophy of Ricardian specialisation, according to which every region exhibits some kind of comparative advantages and should increase its specialisation according to the sectors in which such comparative advantages are likely to be strong. Rather, what matters in smart specialisation is the development of new specialties, through which regional systems will experience structural changes (diversification). Such misunderstanding was certainly a problem at the beginning – hindering regional policy-makers from capturing the true logic of smart specialisation as an evolutionary and dynamic process of structural transformation. In many cases, the building of the smart specialisation strategy was limited to completing a SWOT analysis, providing information about the aspects of the economy that should be strengthened even further. While a SWOT analysis is always a good thing to do, it only provides a guideline and does not necessarily supply any information about the key entrepreneurial discovery processes that can drive the development of new specialties (see Chapter 5 concerning the first lessons drawn from close interactions with certain regions regarding their implantation practice of smart specialisation strategy).

As P. McCann and R. Ortega-Argilés (2013a) suggested in a recent paper, the smart specialisation concept was not primarily related to regions or to regional policy, and in fact the original authors (David, Foray, Hall and van Ark) are not spatial economists or experts in regional policy. Therefore, the initial deployment of the policy concept did not fully take into account the spatial dimension until the mobilisation of spatial economists and regional studies experts greatly contributed to the development of that dimension of the policy process.[9] As a result of their contributions, it became increasingly clear that the *modus operandi* of smart specialisation as policy approach was very much in coherence with the regional policy level and that smart specialisation as a policy tool to generate structural changes was well profiled for regional policymaking.

3 Policy running ahead of theory

The recent rapid success of the term smart specialisation is a pleasing result for the academics at the origin of the concept. However, it is also a perfect example of 'policy running ahead of theory' (Steinmueller, 2010). The idea of smart specialisation has been rapidly adopted by the policy community in spite of a modest theoretical framework to guide its application and a lack of adequate evidence base to help regulate its implementation – a potentially risky course of action. While smart specialisation already seems to be a policy hit and policy-makers have become actively engaged in formulating smart specialisation strategies, the concept is not yet 'tight'[10] – it lacks transparency, verifiability and broad consensus. Many statements and arguments about smart specialisation are not yet based on sound empirical foundations. The good news is that the "theory" is in progress thanks to the research programme of some evolutionary and geographical economists (Boschma, Frenken, Neffke and co-authors) who are building the theory and producing the empirical evidence of industrial and structural changes (origins, effects, measurement) at regional level. This will provide a sound framework for developing more detailed, precise and evidence-based smart specialisation policy prescriptions.

The arc of science: a representation of the intellectual path of the smart specialisation approach

This is the arc of science popularised by P. Romer. It is based on the well-known taxonomy, involving basic and applied research plus the so-called use-inspired basic research – research that is performed for practical reasons but that, for that purpose, needs the advancement of fundamental knowledge. The lesson drawn by Romer (2005) is that science moves forward when it arcs up to a higher level of abstraction and then adds back the details and context necessary to put any new insights to work in the so-called real world.

With this figure Romer described a typical knowledge process that starts from some concrete level of analysis, then strips away context and details to examine the essential elements of the problem before putting the insights gathered from abstract analysis back to work. Many sciences made tremendous progress by trending towards a higher level of abstraction. It is clear that this upward arc is the way scientific progress occurs. However, as this transition is more or less complete, the more likely impediment to further progress is that scientists pay too little attention to the re-entry or landing process that links abstraction back to practice. As Romer (2005) wrote: 'they make the trip up but never come back down!'

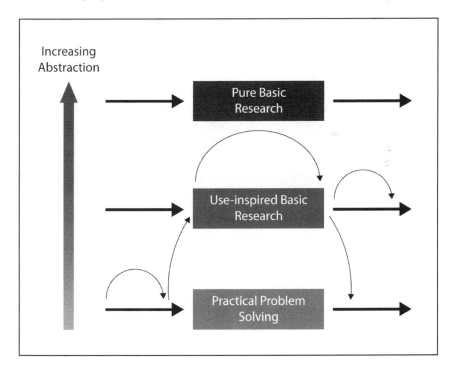

Figure 1.1 The arc of science
Source: Romer, 2005

This is an interesting way to represent the intellectual path of smart specialisation and to show that the journey has not yet been completed.

We started with concrete problems concerning the lack of attractiveness of most regions vis-à-vis the location strategies of multinationals in terms of R&D and innovation. We then eliminated contexts and details to analyse the basic components of the problem and thus discussed, in a more (although not highly) abstract way, the fundamentals of such attractiveness: the development of new specialities, linked with existing productive structures, with a view to extending and strengthening a unique and original knowledge base and diversifying the system. The next challenge was to add back the details and contexts necessary to put any new insights to work in the real world in order to translate the concept of smart specialisation strategy into terms of political prescriptions and then more detailed and precise programmes; in other words, adapting to the operationalisation phase. In short, it is this journey on the arc of science that the reader is now invited to make.

4 Summary of Chapter 1

In this chapter I retraced the origin of the concept of smart specialisation strategy by referring to the works of the *Knowledge for Growth* Expert Group

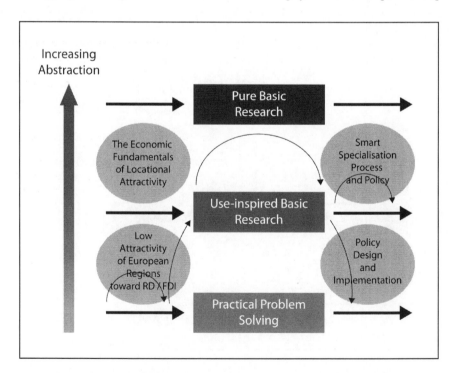

Figure 1.2 Smart specialisation on the arc of science
Source: Adapted from Romer, 2005

between 2005 and 2009. I also emphasised the intellectual progression that has occurred within a wide academic and political community, leading to the notions of regional innovation policies and strategies. In this context, the theoretical and empirical reflections on the role of clusters in innovation and regional cluster policies have dominated debates since the turn of the century. The concept of smart specialisation strategy constitutes both a continuity of and a break with the notion of cluster policy.

Notes

1 This Group was co-chaired by the Commissioner and an academic (B. van Ark and then D. Foray). The Group included P. Aghion, P.A. David, J.P. Fitoussi, M. da Graça de Carvalho, B. Hall, M. Kager, G. Licht, J. Mairesse, R. Marimon, S. Metcalfe, M. Mrak, M. O'Sullivan, A. Sapir, A. Giannitsis and R. Veugelers.
2 http://ec.europa.eu/europe2020/index_en.htm.
3 COM (2011) 615, http://eur-lex.europa.eu/LexUriServ/LexUriServ.do?uri=COM:2 011:0615:FIN:EN:PDF.
4 http://s3platform.jrc.ec.europa.eu. See also the *Guide to Research and Innovation Strategies for Smart Specialisation* (European Commission, 2012a) prepared under the auspices of the RIS3 Platform (http://s3platform.jrc.ec.europa.eu/S3pguide).
5 The contribution of some members of the European Parliament to the diffusion and widespread adoption of the policy concept cannot be left unacknowledged. See, for example, the publication prepared by L. van Nistelrooij (member of European Parliament): *Smart Specialisation: Connecting European Top Performers*, Brussels: Europe Close-by Publications, February 2013.
6 The French business clusters are nothing more than the result of a cluster policy, coordinated at national level: the identification and evaluation of regional strong points that must be reinforced are carried out by the State.
7 See the European Cluster Observatory, which is systematically gathering data on clusters in Europe: www.clusterobservatory.eu.
8 See, inter alia, Jaffe (1989), Jaffe *et al.* (1993), Audretsch and Feldman (1996), and Breschi and Lissoni (2005).
9 See, for example, Barca *et al.* 2012; McCann and Ortega-Argilés, 2013a, 2013b; Ketels, 2013; Morgan, 2013; Camagni *et al.* 2014; Navarro *et al.* 2011; Hildreth and Bailey, 2013. See also two special issues edited by regional science experts, one in *Ekonomiaz* (2013) and the other in *Scienze Regionali* (2014), as well as many articles in recent issues of *European Planning Studies* and the *Cambridge Journal of Regions, Economy and Society.*
10 I borrowed the notion of 'tightness' from Mokyr (2004).

2 From smart specialisation to smart specialisation policy

To clearly understand the concept of smart specialisation policy it is helpful to start thinking about what this concept means as a virtuous process of structural transformations via the discovery and exploration of new domains. Once this process has been thoroughly understood, we can then concern ourselves with the policies that can generate and facilitate it.

1 Smart specialisation dynamics

In many cases the development process leading to smart specialisation can occur in a spontaneous and decentralised way, and with great success. It is triggered by an entrepreneurial vision, the discovery of a new domain and the integration of different types of knowledge to turn this discovery into reality. It is then stimulated by the spillovers generated by this discovery, the entry and agglomeration of firms around the new activity, and then the growth of the latter, allowing structural change (diversification, modernisation, transition). The entrepreneurial discovery, integration of dispersed knowledge, tension between private appropriation logic and spillover logic, and provision of new specific public goods necessary for the growth of the new activity all represent difficulties that are not easily surmountable, and often necessitate the implementation of a public policy. However, the examples below show that this is not always the case.

Smart specialisation stories

Morez: the vision of Pierre-Hyacinthe Cazeaux

This was in 1796 in the region of Morez – a small town on the border between France and Switzerland. Pierre-Hyacinthe Caseaux discovered that from his production of nails he could switch to the production of glasses (spectacles) using the same techniques and capabilities. Soon other nail producers started to manufacture glasses, leading to the creation of many factories within the next 20 years and the opening of a technical school to train apprentices. Morez became a world-class centre for the manufacture of glasses. Indeed, this is a simple story. However, it includes the three main episodes of a smart specialisation process: *entrepreneurial discovery and spillovers* (the discovery is the fact that it is possible to move from nails to glasses on the basis of a similar set of engineering capabilities and techniques); *entry and agglomeration* of similar and complementary businesses (cluster formation); *structural changes* (in the form of the transition from an old business to a new one). This is smart specialisation without policy, like numerous other cases in history.

Marinha Grande: Anibal's travels

In the thirties, Anibal H. Abrantes created the first mould manufacturing company in Portugal, the main market for which was glass-making. However, the latter was in decline and Abrantes very quickly saw the economic potential offered by the new plastic products market. He observed the rapid development of 'plastic firms' in a large number of sectors (toys, electrical equipment, household utensils and articles). He travelled all over Europe and brought back all sorts of plastic products manufactured by injection moulding for which he wanted to design and produce the moulds. He then explored the possibility of a major diversification of his companies by converting the production tooling. This entrepreneurial discovery was to have two effects (Sopas, 2001): providing an exceptional boost to the mould manufacturing industry in which the Marinha Grande cluster still plays a very important role today and encouraging the setting-up of a large number of firms producing plastic articles in the same region. As in Morez, the sequence is infallible and the industrial dynamic very virtuous: entrepreneurial discovery, entry and agglomeration, structural change!

Lyon: the modern Canuts

As a result of a crisis situation faced by traditional markets in the silk industry (that began to decline in the 1960s), a dozen firms broke away from the Lyon factory to explore ways of orchestrating a fundamental transition from silk to technical fabrics (Houssel and Houssel, 1992). They were silk manufacturers who had discovered that the Americans were using glass fibre in the aeronautics sector and these firms worked on the integration of these new materials (glass fibre and then composite materials) into their processes. 'This marriage between textile and chemistry opens the way to a multitude of products for new outlets in aerospace and transport equipment, sports, protection and decoration items, medical prostheses and geotextiles' (Houssel and Houssel, 1992). In the big Lyon chemical complex, firms found the specialists they needed to resolve complex knowledge integration issues relating to the spinning of glass fibre, address warping problems and master the adhesion of the resin to the glass fibre. The nose of the Concorde supersonic airliner, the tail fin of the Airbus 330 and the sails of some of the boats participating in the America's Cup are products symbolising this successful transition. Here again entrepreneurial discovery, agglomeration and structural changes characterise the dynamic that leads to the construction of strong competitive advantages, realised by the creation of over 2,000 jobs between the early 1970s and end of the 1980s.

Finland: pulp and paper companies

In Finland, a group of companies in the pulp and paper industry were exploring the potentials of some new applied science and technologies to improve the operational efficiency of manufacturing processes in this traditional industry (Nikulainen, 2008). A few Finnish entrepreneurs viewed nanotechnology as a promising source of valuable applications and firms in this industry were taking steps to assess this potential. Some firms responded to these opportunities by increasing their R&D spending, exploring recent advances in nanotechnology in order to develop applications for their own sector. The emergence of a new R&D collaboration network – involving incumbents, research institutions, specialised suppliers and universities – was a critical step for the assessment of the usefulness and value of developing nanotechnology applications for pulp and paper processes. Once again we see an entrepreneurial discovery process at work that assembles different actors and will lead to the development of a new activity – at the crossroads between a new technology and a traditional sector – and structural changes (modernisation and diversification).

Basel Region: Small and Medium-sized Enterprises in the Jura and the six surgeons

This is a fifth example of a successful smart specialisation without a policy – an incredible story from the 1960s. Six Swiss surgeons located in the region of Basel and Biel visualised a revolution (Schlich, 2002). This vision concerned new methods to repair broken bones using internal fixations (plates and screws) and early functional exercise. They created the *Arbeitsgemeinschaft für Osteosynthese* (AO) in 1958 to develop and teach the new techniques and practices in Swiss and later European medical schools and hospitals. However, they also needed specialised suppliers to produce top-quality tools and devices – the famous screws, plates, etc. One of the surgeons contacted a young engineer – R. Mathys – who owned a small metal processing factory near Basel. He was convinced to shift its production plan to medical technologies. The connection between the visionary surgeons and the engineer was productive and after two years of development, trials, failures and experiments, Mathys succeeded in becoming the first company to enter this new, fast-growing market. Later, the surgeons contacted a second firm – Straumann, already known for developing sophisticated alloys – to develop the same kind of tools and instruments. At the same time, the surgeons created their own company based in Davos, Switzerland – Synthes – that was responsible for R&D, training and the promotion of the new techniques all over the world. Then a spin-off of Straumann entered the market to develop specific manufacturing processes. The bank also played a role in this emerging ecosystem: after two years of development without any products to sell, Mathys accumulated a debt of 300,000 Swiss francs that worried the local bank. However, the surgeons used their prestige and reputation to convince the bank to extend credit to Mathys. AO, Synthes and the Small and Medium-sized Enterprises (SMEs) supported by the local bank soon achieved incredible success that involved introducing the global medical sphere to a new technique that they collectively controlled!

This last case offers the example of a smart specialisation dynamic that is much more sophisticated than the others. Again, in spite of complex coordination problems, this has been a successful process without any policy. It involved the structuring of entrepreneurial knowledge that was initially fragmented (among surgeons and engineers). It also involved the creation of private institutions to solve important coordination problems that arose as the new activity started to grow.

Simple dynamics and stylised facts

Cases like Morez, Marinha Grande, Lyon, the Finnish pulp and paper industry and the Basel region of successful transformation processes (many of which have one or more elements of a smart specialisation process) are numerous and have been extensively studied in the literature both in the economics of the geography of innovation and regional policy, and in historical studies of technological change (although not under the heading of smart specialisation).

I simplified these five stories to illuminate some stylised facts. They were, of course, more complicated and the production decisions of Caseaux in Morez and others in Lyon, Marinha Grande, Finland or Basel were far less obvious than I have described and these smart specialisation successes were therefore low-probability events and hard to predict. The five stories also vary greatly in their sectoral and geographic contexts, as well as their historical circumstances. However, there are noticeable similarities that in a way represent the common structure of a smart specialisation dynamic.

Entrepreneurial discovery

The fundamental act underlying the described historical dynamics is an entrepreneurial discovery. It precedes the innovation stage and consists of the exploration and establishment of a new domain of opportunities (technological and market), potentially rich in numerous innovations that will subsequently occur.

It is clear that the entrepreneurial discovery, which lies at the origin of each of the historical dynamics presented, does not only amount to innovation[1] – although it increases its probability. It does not simply amount to a basic research phase either as it is essentially oriented towards the market and applications. It is the demonstration that something is possible – for example, moving from the manufacture of nails to glasses; developing from traditional silk manufacture to a production of technical fabrics; integrating nano-technologies into the wood pulp production process; founding a new domain for the treatment of fractures. Entrepreneurial discovery is the essential phase, the decisive link that allows the system to reorient and renew itself. Indeed, the entrepreneurial discovery that drives the process of smart specialisation is not simply the advent of an innovation but the deployment and variation of innovative ideas in a specialised area that generate knowledge about the future economic value of a possible direction of change.

As far as I am aware, the earliest economic conceptualisation of 'discovery', as opposed to innovation, is to be found in the works that Hirshleifer (1971) devoted to knowledge and information. In his works he developed a formal expression of *discovery information* as a compound event A, which consists of the joint happenings: 'state a is true (something is possible)' and 'this fact is successfully exploited (what is possible is created)'. The first event has a probability $\prod a$ while the second event has a probability $\prod A$ with $\prod a > \prod A$. The discovery process provides information about $\prod a$: something is possible that will happen with a probability $\prod A$.

The discovery A may be about the potential of a *general purpose technology application to transform processes* in a traditional sector (the case of pulp and paper). Or it may be about the possibility of a *diversification path based on the exploitation of potential economies of scope and internal spillovers* (the case of plastics firms that diversify their products from the car industry to new markets, as in the Basque Country, Spain, or the Midlands region of the United Kingdom). Or the discovery is about the possibility of a *transition path from a low-productivity area to a higher one* (from traditional silk to technical materials in Lyon; or from metal processing to medical technologies for the Swiss SMEs).[2]

All these cases do indeed describe entrepreneurial explorations, experiments and discoveries (not simple innovations) that concern either i) the complementarity between a general purpose technology (or a key enabling technology) application and a traditional sector[3]; or ii) potential economies of scope between two different lines of business that can stimulate a diversification process; or iii) a transition path from an existing set of collective capabilities to the foundations of a new business. An entrepreneurial discovery is a new area of structural change that opens up, into which a whole segment of an industry can move to explore it and generate numerous innovations.

Entrepreneurial knowledge and economic knowledge

The various stories presented above place the notion of entrepreneurial knowledge at the centre of the process. Entrepreneurial knowledge – composed of vision and integration between different bodies of knowledge – plays an essential role in the discovery of a new domain; it is the driver of the discovery process. Entrepreneurial knowledge involves much more than knowledge about science and techniques. Rather, it combines and relates such knowledge about science, technology and engineering with knowledge of market growth potential, potential competitors as well as the whole set of inputs and services required for launching a new activity. From the policy point of view that will be introduced later in this chapter, entrepreneurial knowledge is thus a precious input to generate relevant information during the priority-setting process.

It would be a mistake to think that the entrepreneurial discovery process generates only technological knowledge – what works from a technological point of view. On the contrary, the discovery focuses on economic knowledge – the knowledge of what works (and does not work) economically, as elaborated by Hayek (1978) and which is central to the general theory of economic dynamism developed by Phelps (2013). The entrepreneurial discovery process is basically economic experimentation with new ideas, which, of course, will emanate to a great extent from scientific and technological inventions.

Figure 2.1 presents and links both types of knowledge within the entrepreneurial discovery framework: entrepreneurial knowledge, which must be

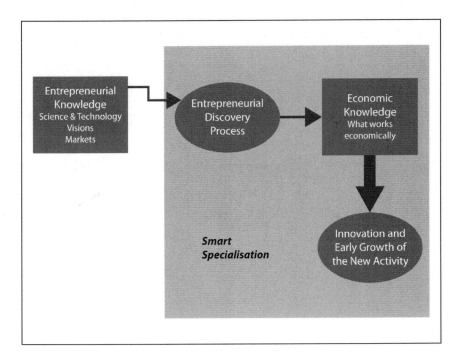

Figure 2.1 Types of knowledge and the entrepreneurial discovery process

mobilised and integrated as an input of the discovery process, and economic knowledge, which represents the output of this discovery process.

Let's take a rather extraordinary example to illustrate Figure 2.1 and show that science and technology do not necessarily play an essential role in the entrepreneurial discovery process, whereas entrepreneurial and economic knowledge is always central. It is the story of a businessman who buys a small airport in Wales with the hope of turning it into an airport for private jets and business flights.[4] The market unfortunately does not respond. He then *discovers* the possibility of converting this airport into a pilot installation and test centre for unmanned aerial vehicles (UAVs) or drones. With the support of the Welsh Assembly, the installations are developed to offer a range of technological services for the R&D and operational flights of UAVs. A small cluster is formed composed of high-tech firms specialising in military aircraft markets. The next discovery will no doubt be brought about by the emergence of a civil UAV market. Here is a surprising smart specialisation dynamic in which entrepreneurial vision and discovery produced economic knowledge concerning the unforeseen viability of a new speciality for the Cardigan Bay region in Wales.

Another case from Portugal will help to illustrate the process of structuration of entrepreneurial knowledge and the subsequent developments (entrepreneurial discovery, economic experimentation and smart specialisation) as represented in Figure 2.1. This case is that of the footwear industry, which has undergone profound renewal in a context of frantic global competition. The entrepreneurial knowledge enabling the development of new forms of flexible automation in the footwear industry in Portugal is based on integration of engineering knowledge from the University of Porto (INESC), skills of companies specialised in industrial machinery, tools and software and the entrepreneurial vision of a few footwear manufacturing firms which understand very well the urgent need for revival via innovation. The integration of this knowledge facilitates the discovery and exploration of the potential of the automation associated with advanced cutting tools to increase the flexibility and quality of production. Economic experimentation with these technological developments determines a new business model. The latter is based on an increase in the variety of models and the capacity to rapidly respond to small orders. This development has led the footwear industry to bypass global competition and become the second most important European producer in terms of exportation and added value.

The locus of entrepreneurial discovery

The processes of entrepreneurial discovery and exploration of new domains of potential innovations usually require the integration of divided and dispersed knowledge (see Box 2.1). This is why the organisational forms most appropriate for entrepreneurial discovery are the network, association or partnership, forms allowing the integration of knowledge originating from firms, research laboratories, specialised suppliers and clients. The research laboratory-backed start-up falls into this category, of course. We also observe the presence of more horizontal associations, allowing, for example, the collaboration of small firms that share certain infrastructures and services for the collective exploration of a new domain.

However, the large integrated company is also a possible locus since it is by definition capable of assembling diversified knowledge and carrying out risky discovery projects by financing its projects with its own resources. In her recent work, S. Berger gives numerous examples of German companies that create new industries through an internal entrepreneurial discovery process:

> What (we) saw in company after company was the repurposing of key technologies to develop wholly new products and services .... New businesses are being created, not usually through start-ups – in contrast to the American model – but through the transformation of old capabilities and their reapplication and repurposing for new ends
>
> (Berger, 2013: pp. 134–37).

Berger's book is brimming with examples of companies, moving from autos to solar modules, from semiconductors to solar cells, or from machines to make spark plugs to machines that make medical devices like artificial knees (Berger, 2013: p. 137). These are illuminating cases of entrepreneurial knowledge structuring (often thanks to relations between the large company and one of its clients that poses a very specific industrial problem), exploration of the new domain (for example, the application of core wet chemistry technologies to solar cell equipment), and economic knowledge production (via the implementation of new equipment at the client company) (Berger, 2013: p. 134). The organisational characteristics of the large integrated company enable all this to be accomplished.

Therefore, numerous organisational forms are possible for integrating divided and dispersed knowledge and managing the risks of entrepreneurial discovery projects, from the research laboratory-backed start-up to the large integrated firm, and all sorts of forms of networks in between.

Spillovers and entry of similar or complementary businesses

Discoveries are characterised by a strong learning dimension. The social value of the discovery is that it informs the whole system that a particular domain of R&D and innovation is likely to create new opportunities for the regional economy. This is not the standard model, whereby an innovator excludes others from the use of the innovation in order to appropriate the largest fraction of the benefits. Discoveries and subsequent emerging activities have the potential to provide learning spillovers to other agents in the regional economy. Thus, as Rodrik (2004) argues, the reward for entrepreneurial discoveries (if it is needed, i.e. in case of informational externality problems) has to be structured in such a way that it will maximise these spillovers.

While entrepreneurial discovery signifies the opening up of exploitation opportunities, entry constitutes the confirmation that others see this discovery as meaningful. When the initial experiment and discovery are successful and diffused, other agents are induced to shift investments away from older domains with less growth potential to the new one. According to Hirshleifer (1971), public information about the discovery (about $\prod a$) is socially valuable in redirecting productive decisions. Entry is a key ingredient of smart specialisation so that agglomeration externalities can be realised: the discovery of a potential domain in which a region could become a leader should quickly result in multiple entrants to the new activity. This is the onset of the clustering phase of a smart specialisation process, i.e. the formation of regional concentration of co-located activities and resources in related fields.

Structural changes and related variety

The potential success of discoveries and new activities that aim to explore and open up a new area of opportunities will ultimately translate into some kind of structural changes within the economy.[5] The outcome of the process is thus much more than a 'simple' technological innovation, but rather a structural evolution of the whole regional economy. Different logics of structural transformations can be identified:

- Transition is characterised by a new domain emerging from an existing industrial commons (a collection of R&D, engineering and manufacturing capabilities that sustain innovation). The case of silk/textile firms in Lyon exemplifies such a transition pattern from traditional technologies for old declining markets to new technologies allowing these firms to enter new markets.
- Modernisation is manifested when the development of specific applications of a general purpose technology produces a significant impact on the efficiency and quality of an existing (often traditional) sector. A good case in point is the example, mentioned above, of the development of nanotechnology applications to improve processes and products in the pulp and paper industry. There are many other examples, such as the development of ICT applications in tourism and the exploration of biotechnology potentials in the agrofood industry. In all these instances, the intersection between the development of applications of a general purpose technology and a mature sector defines a space of opportunities in which entrepreneurs' experiments and discoveries can be expected to produce socially useful knowledge.
- Diversification, in a narrow sense, is a third pattern. In such cases the discovery concerns potential synergies (economies of scope) that are likely to materialise between an existing activity and a new one. Such synergies

make the move towards a new, growing market attractive and profitable. Our example of the plastic firms in the Basque Country is a good case in point.

We see from the three first patterns that the essence of entrepreneurial discovery and the development of subsequent new activities involves exploring the *adjacent possible*, to borrow a scientific analogy. The *adjacent possible* captures both the present limits of and the potential for innovation and transformation of the existing structures.

- Radical foundation is a fourth pattern. In this case, a new domain is founded with no direct link with existing structures.

It is important to have some sort of typology of structural changes in mind because it will provide policy-makers with the possibility to think ahead – looking at my regional economy, where, in or between which sectors, are structural changes most desirable? – and will produce information concerning the kind of domains or sectors in which entrepreneurial discovery could be socially valuable (see Chapter 3).

We can see from the cases above that, in general, entrepreneurial discoveries relate to existing structures and local knowledge. Modernisation, diversification and transition are forms of evolution whose point of departure is existing productive capabilities, which are determined by local technological and productive contexts and stimulated by the integration of new knowledge. Each of these cases exemplify processes of transformation that link the existing productive structures to new domains of potential competitive advantages. All these cases involve the generation of related variety (Frenken *et al.* 2007; Aghion *et al.* 2009; Boschma and Frenken, 2009).

Related variety is the fundamental logic of translating entrepreneurial discovery and subsequent new activity into structural change. This means that technological contexts matter for evolution in terms of pathways for innovation. As a result, 'regions diversify by branching into industries that are related to their current industries' (Neffke *et al.* 2009).

However, the fourth pattern is different in this respect. It involves the less frequent case of the radical foundation of a new domain. This case does not fall into the related diversification pattern and involves the opening up of exploitation opportunities unrelated to any existing productive assets.

Made in Switzerland!

The case from Switzerland recounted above is a good illustration that in the absence of market failure smart specialisation is likely to happen successfully without a policy. The example was about entrepreneurial discovery, but the initial entrepreneurial knowledge was dispersed among surgeons and metalworking SMEs. The surgeons played a crucial role.[6] They realised the integration of the dispersed entrepreneurial knowledge. Moreover, they supported spillovers, entry and agglomeration. Indeed, they developed a fine policy concerning intellectual property rights: the patents that protected the inventions of the special instruments and implants developed by AO surgeons or the manufacturers were all transferred to Synthes, which then granted the right of exclusive production and marketing of the AO equipment. Synthes also produced the new, activity-specific public goods (R&D, training and quality standards). Thanks to AO and the entrepreneurial spirit of the SMEs, the emerging ecosystem has been remarkable in building connections to integrate the dispersed knowledge and realise the entrepreneurial discovery process, as well as producing a private institution (Synthes). Synthes was founded to solve the coordination problems arising from the early growth of the new activity, to support capability formation and to reward the pioneers in such a way that spillovers were maximised (Schlich, 2002).

It is clear therefore that the classic market failures (knowledge externalities, uncertainty, access to finance, as well as the provision of industry-specific public goods, see Box 2.1) were not present here or were spontaneously corrected through the operation of the private institution created by the surgeons.[7] Hence, no policy was needed to support the entrepreneurial discovery process and the early growth of the new activities. Smart specialisation was successfully achieved, creating strong competitive advantages for many decades – and this was attained without any dedicated policy beyond the production of strong framework conditions.

Box 2.1 Market and coordination failures in a smart specialisation process

The potential presence of strong market and coordination failures characterising the economic environment of a smart specialisation process is likely to result both in systemic under-investment in entrepreneurial discoveries, lower than socially desirable rates of discoveries, and in obstacles and difficulties of development and early growth of the new activities, once the discovery has been made.

Entrepreneurial knowledge division and dispersion: the division of knowledge stems from division of labour and increasing specialisation in the field of knowledge production. Its dispersion is related to local situations in which knowledge is produced. The result is an extremely fragmented knowledge base (Foray, 2004: p. 18; Machlup, 1984; Minkler, 1993). The integration of dispersed and divided knowledge creates an externality that is a source of market failure (see the *weak appropriability* case below).

Weak appropriability of entrepreneurial discovery: the discovery of new domains of opportunities entails significant information externalities that are virtually impossible to appropriate, causing a wide gap between social and private returns to discoveries (Nelson, 1959; Arrow, 1962; Trajtenberg, 2012). Note that the usual solution involving the use of intellectual property rights is not appropriate here since the information spillovers need to be maximised (see Hirshleifer's argument, above). Thus, the appropriability problem is even more severe in the case of discovery than in the case of 'simple' innovation (for which the use of a patent is a plausible – although second-best – solution).

Uncertainty: the value of a discovery is more conjectural than that of applied research and other innovation-related activities and is therefore more likely to be undervalued by firms; the variance of distribution of expected returns from discoveries is much higher (Arrow, 1962; Dasgupta, 1988).

Access to finance: an additional gap exists between the private rate of return required by an entrepreneur and the cost of capital when the entrepreneur and financier are different entities (Hall and Lerner, 2010).

Increasing returns in the form of agglomeration economies (including large firms' spin-off externalities, anchor tenant externalities and small firms' externalities – Agrawal and Cockburn, 2003; Agrawal, Cockburn and Oettl, 2010) are a generic source of market failures.

Coordination failures: a lot of coordination problems may arise from the early growth stage of the new activity with the need for simultaneous investment in various segments of the activity (Rodrik, 2004), as well as the provision of new industry-specific public goods (Romer, 1993).

2 From smart specialisation process to policy

The Swiss case is likely to be an exception and in most cases market failures will block the process of entrepreneurial discoveries. It often does not work so well and several problems may be encountered.

The notion of entrepreneurial discovery lies at the heart of the smart specialisation logic. Yet, entrepreneurial discoveries may not be produced in sufficient quantity for reasons of imperfect appropriability, lack of capabilities and difficult credit access. Discovery, if successful, launches the development of a new speciality aimed at transforming the system; however, this speciality may remain sub-critical in terms of scale, network, clusters, complementary investments and specific public goods for numerous reasons stemming from coordination failures. Resources must then be concentrated on a small number of new activities, which will therefore be priorities, in order to reach the critical thresholds and minimum efficiency scale that will allow these activities to develop.

The processes in Morez, Lyon or the Basel region might be an exception and the key policy question is therefore to ask what are the structural conditions and policies in a given region that will increase the likelihood of such events and that there will be a good number of experiments and discoveries – some giving rise to real solid drivers for regional economic growth. While cases of smart specialisation processes without a policy do exist, in many instances market and coordination failures make policies indispensable.

I hope that I have made it clear that smart specialisation as a process of evolution is not at all new. However, a policy aimed at promoting smart specialisation does have some new elements. I will discuss these new elements here, as well as in Chapter 3.

3 Graphical representation of a smart specialisation policy in Region X

I can provide a graphical representation of what is at stake with a smart specialisation policy. Why do I think that smart specialisation can make a difference vis-à-vis the older horizontal policies? Let's take Region X, not particularly well advanced, and I shall construct a measure of knowledge convergence – some kind of composite index including several indicators concerning higher education, scientific publications, patent intensity, R&D intensity, venture capital, etc. In recent decades, the region has devoted most of its resources to horizontal policies – i.e. policies aimed at improving general framework conditions and targeting 'whole populations' (of firms or people) to upgrade capabilities. However, the results are somewhat discouraging.

There is still a significant knowledge gap between this region and the leading ones. This is what the first evaluation exercises regarding the effect of Structural Funds in research, technological development and innovation

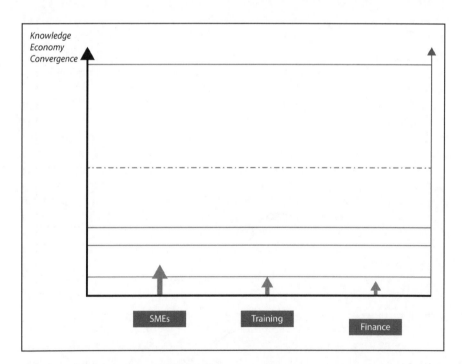

Figure 2.2 Horizontal policy in Region X

(RTDI) for the period 2000–09 have shown: no significant contribution of this policy to economic growth (Muscio *et al.* 2013).[8] The most recent empirical research has also found no effect of horizontal policies on individuals' start up intentions and engagement during start-up activities (Stuetzer *et al.* 2014).

Of course these horizontal policies need to be continued through European as well as national programmes, but in addition to these policies, Region X is implementing a smart specialisation strategy and prioritises two, three or more new activities, and these new activities – owing to resource concentration as well as a proper method to identify and select them – will approach the frontier of knowledge convergence.

What are the three things that have been prioritised? There are new *discovery activities* (R&D and innovation) that complement existing structures and assets. They are likely to generate *informational spillovers* on the feasibility and future value of certain paths of *structural change* through R&D and innovation in an important sector (or at the intersection between sectors) of the regional economy. By way of explanation, the first activity involves the connection between a public laboratory specialising in animal genetics, a strong, high-quality but traditional breeding sector and some specialised suppliers of technological solutions. The aim of this first activity is to shift an

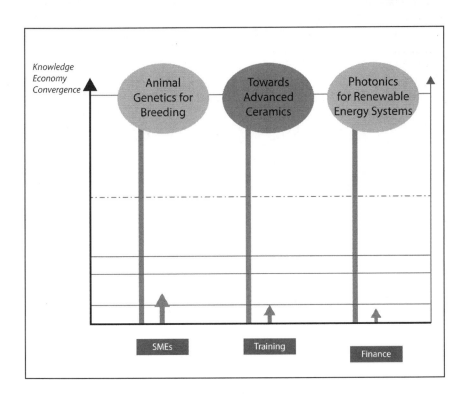

Figure 2.3 Smart specialisation strategy in Region X

important traditional sector into the modern part of the economy by integrating into the former the appropriate scientific knowledge. The second activity involves a group of firms belonging to the traditional ceramics sector, which want to explore a new domain of diversification through the development of advanced ceramics – a development that will allow these firms to target new market niches. The third activity emerges from a high-tech cluster and is about the development of advanced photonics in the area of new renewable energy.

Between Figure 2.2 and Figure 2.3, several things have happened: a structuring process of entrepreneurial knowledge, a discovery procedure and the constitution of scales or organisation of a critical mass of resources.

Structuring entrepreneurial knowledge

Entrepreneurial knowledge is the critical input in the discovery process (see Figure 2.1). In some of the cases presented above (Morez, Lyon, Marinha Grande, the Basel region, pulp and paper in Finland), entrepreneurial knowledge is generated, structured and developed spontaneously by the actors themselves, allowing entrepreneurial discovery projects to be accomplished without the need for any other policy than the one that ensures the consolidation of framework conditions.

However, these cases are perhaps exceptional. Entrepreneurial knowledge is fragmented and dispersed; it is not available in compact form within one single entity (Bresnahan, 2012). Some elements of this knowledge are also likely to be located elsewhere. Entrepreneurial knowledge is not necessarily located in high-tech companies; firms, local universities and public laboratories, medical schools and hospitals, public services, and communities of practices are also possible repositories of elements of relevant entrepreneurial knowledge.

The scarcity and fragmentation of entrepreneurial knowledge as well as its uncertain locatability create a strong case for policy intervention in order to support the generation and/or integration of the knowledge needed for entrepreneurial discoveries and the development of subsequent new activities. Furthermore, numerous factors – that can be grouped under the title of market failures – can prevent a sufficient number of entrepreneurial experiments from being carried out in certain domains or even in the entire regional economy (see Box 2.1). Therefore, the main questions for policy-makers are: who has, or where is, the entrepreneurial knowledge? How can the fragmented knowledge base be integrated so as to generate exploration and discovery projects? This is demonstrated by what occurs between Figure 2.2 and Figure 2.3.

I will show in Chapter 3 and Chapter 4 that a critical policy task involves the mobilisation of available entrepreneurial knowledge as well as the construction and integration of the entrepreneurial knowledge that is dispersed and distributed among several entities.

A problem of identification and discovery

As already stressed in the introduction, the identification and selection of new activities forms an integral part of the policy process. While the identification of actions of a horizontal policy does not give rise to too many problems (see Figure 2.2), the selection of new activities in a vertical policy logic is far more difficult. The information necessary for prioritisation must come from entrepreneurial discoveries made by firms, laboratories and specialised services based on the integration of their knowledge. The discoveries and new activities identified in Figure 2.3 have been considered to be potentially rich in spillovers, innovations and structural changes, thanks to the *ex-ante* evaluation of these projects within the context of intense and continual interactions between government and industry (see the nine evaluation criteria proposed in Box 3.2). This is also demonstrated by what occurs between Figure 2.2 and Figure 2.3.

The constitution of scales and the generation of critical masses of resources will then be organized and the policy process will manage the transition from the entrepreneurial discovery phase to the increasing returns (clustering) phase. As a result of resource concentration, as well as the absorption of knowledge and competences from outside, these new activities are likely soon to move towards the frontier in terms of knowledge convergence (see Figure 2.3).

This is the main idea: having this vertical policy schema in addition to the horizontal programmes in order to enable a region to diversify through the development and consolidation of new specialities or new activities that will facilitate the transformation, revival and renewal of productive structures and generate spillovers towards the rest of the local economy.

4 The great challenge of policy design

A 'new' process of resource allocation: not horizontal but vertical priorities

It is clear that we are not talking here of *horizontal priorities*, such as improving human capital, accelerating transfer of technologies, creating incubators, upgrading SME capabilities or having good universities, but of *vertical priorities* regarding some specific fields, technologies, and perhaps companies.

The change of logic – from horizontal to vertical – can be justified almost negatively by the incapacity of recent horizontal policies to shift a large number of regions into the knowledge economy (Muscio *et al.* 2013; Percoco 2013). This does not mean that these policies must be rejected – we don't know what would happen to these regions without them. It simply means that we cannot rely on these policies alone and that a more vertical, targeted and preferential intervention logic – to concentrate resources on a few new activities originating from a decentralised and well-conducted entrepreneurial discovery process – must be tested.

The goal is therefore to favour the emergence and development of a few 'innovation microsystems' dealing with particular market niches and mostly related to existing productive structures and assets in order to transform them through R&D and innovation (structural changes).

Avoiding distortions and government failures

We now need to respond to all of the usual criticisms and questions that mainstream economics would raise against the case of a *non-neutral* policy. For instance, A. Krueger, commenting on the works of J. Yfu Lin, a great promoter of the new structural economics framework, writes:

> Although it is certainly true that not everything can be done at once, focus on selected areas for large investments to the neglect of the rest of the economy is a highly questionable strategy. Why it would be preferable to allocate scarce capital so that some activities have excellent infrastructures while others must manage with seriously deficient structure is not clear: without further evidence, it would appear to be a distortion.
>
> (Krueger, 2012: p. 224)

Krueger would have plausibly expressed the same objections to smart specialisation policy. Krueger is part of a large group of economists who accept the need for industrial policy, but strongly argue that intervention has to be limited to horizontal and non-neutral interventions and not extended to preferential policies that discriminate across activities.[9]

The difficult policy challenge facing smart specialisation is therefore to emphasise the vertical logic of prioritisation, while avoiding the government failures usually associated with the top-down and centralised bureaucratic processes of technology choices and selection. How can one prioritise and favour some R&D and technological activities, some sub-systems or fields, while not dissipating the extraordinary power of market-driven resource allocation in boosting decentralised entrepreneurial experiments? Vertical prioritisation is difficult; this is why smart specialisation is about defining a method to help policy-makers to identify desirable areas for innovation policy intervention.

These questions are not 'simply' academic. They are particularly topical in policy circles and business communities, as demonstrated by the number of recent articles published on this subject in *The Economist*.[10]

Smart specialisation and the new industrial policy agenda

This kind of question obviously lies at the heart of the agenda of the so-called *New Industrial Policy* developed in particular by Rodrik (2004, 2007), Hausmann and Rodrik (2003), Trajtenberg (2002, 2012), as well as Aghion (2012) and Aghion *et al.* (2011). One item on this agenda is reconciling vertical priority-setting (perhaps sectoral policy in Aghion's view) and a decentralised innovation economy according to W. Baumol or E.S. Phelps, i.e. acknowledging the fact that innovation needs to come from grass roots and not from the top. Indeed the policy design presented below was greatly inspired by Rodrik's thoughts on development economics and policy.

According to the intellectual logic of this *New Industrial Policy* school, smart specialisation can be viewed both as a *policy objective,* to encourage regions and countries to take risks in selecting a few priorities, and a *process,* to help policy-makers identify domains and activities for potential specialisation. This process – the design of smart specialisation strategy – will be explained in detail in Chapter 3.

5 Summary of Chapter 2

This chapter focused on the distinction between smart specialisation – as a worthy dynamic of the development of new specialities that can emerge spontaneously in the economy – and smart specialisation strategy (or policy) – a notion that involves putting in place a policy process aimed at facilitating this dynamic when it cannot develop spontaneously. The chapter began with the analysis of spontaneous smart specialisation dynamics, the presentation of historical examples and the formulation of stylised facts (entrepreneurial discovery, spillovers, entry and agglomeration, structural change and related variety). Next I studied in what conditions a smart specialisation policy is necessary. I then presented a simple graphic case of smart specialisation policy before concluding with the problems that this policy must overcome (entrepreneurial knowledge structuring, identification and discovery, and local resource concentration and distortions).

Notes

1 Baumol (2002) has written extensively on the corporate procedures in routinised innovation, analysing them as both a manifestation of the transformation of the innovation process and central feature of oligopolistic rivalry.
2 These examples are taken from the following case studies respectively: Nikulainen, 2008; Navarro *et al.* 2011; Bailey and MacNeil, 2009; Houssel and Houssel, 1992; Schlich, 2002.
3 I will discuss the centrality of general purpose technology in some patterns of smart specialisation in Chapter 4.
4 See 'Roger, West Wales', *The Economist,* 13 October 2012.
5 For a general theory of relationships between innovation and structural changes, see for example Antonelli (2002).
6 According to Rosenberg's (1995a, 1995b) predictions about surgeons' centrality in the process of innovation in medical technologies.
7 See Weder and Grubel (1993) for a general argument on private institutions (instead of government subsidies) that can capture externalities in research and correct coordination failures.
8 Veugelers and Mrak (2009) analyse the poor performance of the 'catching-up Member States' (i.e. Greece, Portugal, Spain, Ireland, Slovenia, Romania,

Bulgaria, Poland, Hungary, Slovakia, Estonia, Lithuania, Latvia and the Czech Republic) with respect to their knowledge economy convergence.

9 Rodrik (2007) proposes an interesting argument about this school of thought: horizontal interventions are a limiting case more than a clear-cut alternative to sectoral policies. In fact few interventions are truly horizontal. They almost necessarily favour some activities, even if the main goal was not to create such discrimination. This is consistent with Foray (2009) and Foray *et al.* (2012), arguing that much of the discourse of economic policy making has been radically out of step with reality. They support something (namely neutral R&D policies that address market failures and do not favour one sector or technology over others) that does not really exist. Trajtenberg (2012), who is generally in favour of neutral instruments, recognises the need for targeting where there is a negative correlation between (high) social returns and (low) private returns. However, such a possibility of targeting is conditional on the ability of policy-makers to identify, *ex ante,* such negative correlations in specific fields.

10 See *The Economist* articles, including *Tinker, tailor: economists reconsider the merits of industrial policy, but some flaws are hard to fix*, 1 October 2011; *Industrial design: can governments help revive innovation and trade?*, 1 October 2009; *Work to be done: How the government can help things along*, 31 March 2010; *Picking winners, saving losers: Industrial policy is back in fashion. Have governments learned from past failures?* 5 August 2010.

3 Designing a smart specialisation strategy

The central insight underlying smart specialisation policy is that, beyond the horizontal programmes that are essential to improve framework conditions and general capabilities, it is crucial to set priorities. Resources should be concentrated in specially selected domains dealing with particular kinds of technology, fields, disciplines, and sub-systems within a sector or at the interstices of different sectors.

Chapter 2 emphasised some principles for designing a policy process as well as the general objectives of smart specialisation. From these initial insights some important specific policy proposals can be derived that will contribute to moving a regional system towards smart specialisation. At least five policy design principles are important. They have been conceptualised and studied, to some extent, in the *New Industrial Policy* literature (Rodrik, 2004, 2007; Hausmann and Rodrik, 2003; Aghion *et al.*, 2011; Trajtenberg, 2002, 2012) but have not yet been integrated within a unique framework to address the problems of smart specialisation strategies. The five principles are concerned with:

- solving the identification problem and creating the structural conditions to increase the likelihood of entrepreneurial discovery;
- building an inclusive strategy;
- implementing a process to evaluate and select emerging activities and to assess *ex post* progress;
- determining an exit provision after a certain period of time has elapsed and a mechanism to support a continuous process of discovery and prioritisation; and
- addressing the many coordination failures that are likely to prevent emerging trends from becoming real and solid drivers for regional economic growth.

The details of all these programmes, as well as the relative importance of each, would have to be adjusted based on a more thorough prior analysis of the local context and circumstances of the region considered. For example, if we just consider the simple typology of regions used by the European Commission – more developed/transition/less developed[1] – it is fairly clear that the more developed regions (at least the best of them) can be qualified as 'rich in entrepreneurial discoveries' and in such cases the emphasis of the policy should be on observation, information aggregation and evaluation. On the other hand, the less developed regions can be characterised by weak industry structures and poor entrepreneurial capabilities, and thus the emphasis should be on capability formation so as to increase the rate of entrepreneurial discovery within the regional system (see Chapter 4 and Chapter 5).

In this chapter the description of programmes remains at quite a generic level. In Chapter 4 specific issues and challenges for different types of regions will be addressed, while Chapter 5 will deal with more practical implementation problems.[2]

1 Design principle n° 1: entrepreneurial discoveries and granularity

As already stated in the previous chapter, successful smart specialisation dynamics are rooted in an entrepreneurial discovery process and in many cases government intervention is needed to address the problems of under-investment in entrepreneurial discovery or insufficient capabilities to undertake entrepreneurial discoveries.

Summing up

From a policy point of view, the importance of entrepreneurial discovery lies in fact in the association of two words: *entrepreneurial* and *discovery*.

Entrepreneurial ...

Priorities will be identified where and when opportunities are discovered by entrepreneurs. Prioritisation is no longer the role of the omniscient planner but involves an interactive process in which entrepreneurs are discovering and producing information about new activities, and the government assesses potential and then empowers those actors who are more capable of realising that potential. Entrepreneurs in the broadest sense (innovative firms, research leaders in higher education institutions, independent inventors and innovators) are in the best position to discover the domains of R&D and innovation in which a region is likely to excel, given its existing capabilities and productive assets. This principle, which comes from Hausmann and Rodrik (2003), allows a clear-cut distinction between smart specialisation and older policy style that involved centralised planning methods for identifying priorities.

There is a long history of policies setting priorities and objectives that were very much top-down, centralised and bureaucratic, but they generated a lot of inefficiencies – this is the argument of A. Krueger (see Chapter 2). Entrepreneurial discovery, however, is a unique concept in that it reconciles the idea that policies take things in hand again by shaping the regional system through setting priorities and the idea that market processes are central in producing information about the best domains for future priorities.

... discovery

I am talking of entrepreneurial *discovery*, not entrepreneurial *innovation*. The distinction between 'innovation' and 'discovery' is central. What will need to be identified and supported as vertical priorities are not 'simple' innovations undertaken by individual firms. Horizontal policies are just designed to subsidise the costs of R&D and innovation and incentivise any potential innovator and good project. Vertical policies need to target activities aimed at exploring, experimenting and learning about what should be done in the future within one sector or between different sectors in terms of R&D and innovation. Entrepreneurial discovery precedes the stage of innovation and as such the incentive structures supporting the former will be different from those supporting the latter.

Entrepreneurial discovery and the policy space

It should be clear that the emphasis on entrepreneurial discovery as a decentralised and bottom-up process of producing information about potential priorities should not result in a narrowing of the scope of policy intervention. Emphasising the role of entrepreneurial discovery is not a plea in favour of a *laissez-faire* policy and the constraints I have placed on the process should not result in some kind of shrinkage of policy scope to exclude all governmental actions as being too top-down. Futhermore, the familiar top-down/bottom-up dichotomy is itself not overly helpful in capturing the complexity of the policy process, and policy programmes fostering smart specialisation need to be more sophisticated than the confines of this dichotomy will allow. Putting it candidly, the emphasis on entrepreneurial discovery as the main process for generating information to identify priorities means that the policy is not about telling people what to do, but rather about helping stakeholders to discover what to do and then implementing the necessary sequence of policies according to what has been discovered.[3]

Granularity (new activities)

The level at which those priorities are identified, assessed and supported is neither the sectoral level nor the individual/firm level. The granularity level should not be too high, otherwise smart specialisation transforms itself into a sectoral prioritisation and, as stressed many times, there is no rationale to prioritise *sectors* in terms of innovation policy. Sectoral-level prioritisation is what old-fashioned industrial policy did, based on a weak and controversial rationale, particularly in the area of innovation policy.[4] Sectoral prioritisation for innovation means that all firms in – say – the textile industry are eligible for support just because they are members of this industry. This is nonsense and creates a distortion. Only those textile firms committed to undertaking new and risky projects should be supported.

However, intervention at too detailed a level would transform smart specialisation into a horizontal policy through which all micro-projects of any merit would be supported (a task usually fulfilled by R&D tax credit systems or programmes of R&D subsidies targeting the whole population of firms).

The relevant level is that of 'mid-grained' granularity. At this level:

- new activities/projects involve groups of firms and other (research) partners;
- the aim is to explore a new domain of (technological and market) opportunities;
- there is potentially a certain weight and a high significance in relation to the regional economy (in terms of the kind of structural changes it is likely to generate).

An example is the companies exploring the potentials of nanotechnology to improve the operational efficiency of the pulp and paper industry (Finland). In this case, the priority is not the pulp and paper sector as a whole, but rather the activity involving the development of nanotechnology applications for the pulp and paper industry. In the case of plastics firms exploring diversification from the car industry to biomedical innovations (as in the Basque Country), it is not the plastics industry that is prioritised as such but the activity of exploring diversification opportunities towards biomedical applications. In the case of automotive subcontractors exploring diversification towards new sectors (for example, in the Midlands region of the United Kingdom), again what should be prioritised is not the whole subcontracting sector but the activity of exploring a transition path from the car industry towards new markets.

What governments would support in these cases is neither whole sectors nor single firms but the growth of *new activities*. The notion of a *new activity* is somewhat unclear. Of course economic activities take place at firm level, but the essence of smart specialisation – as well as of any kind of new industrial policy – is not to favour one particular firm but to support *the development of collective action and experience aimed at exploring, experimenting with and discovering new opportunities*.

It is also important to identify the right level between sectors and individual entities at which to assess potentials and determine priorities. Sceptics may say of smart specialisation strategy: yes, it is a generous idea to try to place regions in a top position in the knowledge economy, but is it realistic? Are there enough 'roles' in the knowledge economy 'play'? Is there any risk that some regions will not get a share of the knowledge economy even if they are willing to commit to a smart specialisation strategy? At sector level, this is a relevant question. After all, there are not so many sectors and not all regions can become a global leader in aeronautics or medical instruments. However, when we move to a mid-grained level, the picture is different and much more encouraging. There are lots of things to do in terms of knowledge development and innovations. There is indeed a role for every region. Mid-grained granularity is the right level at which to see in detail the pieces of the knowledge economy that a region can take as a basis for its smart specialisation strategy.

This is also the level at which cooperation opportunities instead of competition constraints can emerge. For example, take a region that has some aeronautic activities while the neighbouring region is a giant in aeronautics. Should the first region find a priority in aeronautics? If we assess potentials at sectoral level, the response is clearly that it should not. However, at a more fine-grained level of observation, we will see a very different picture: the aeronautic activity in the first region, though small, is specific and distinct from what the giant is doing. This small activity involves strong Small and Medium-sized Enterprises (SMEs), a global leader and many R&D activities corresponding to a market niche and is in fact benefiting from productive connections with the giant. Thus, once again, the mid-grained level of (new) activities is the right level for assessment and observation.[5]

Programmes to maximise entrepreneurial discoveries

This step involves many issues and potential policy actions: subsidising the cost of discovery, broadening the space where entrepreneurial knowledge should be sought and activated, mobilising extra-regional capabilities to complement local assets (extra-regional enterprises can initiate and operate new companies in regions where these factors are scarce), creating connections to integrate highly dispersed entrepreneurial knowledge, influencing (targeting) some areas where experiments and discoveries are likely to have strong structural change effects. I will now discuss the most important of these actions based on a couple of well-known market and coordination failures that in many cases will hamper the process of entrepreneurial discovery.

Information externalities

In the recent literature addressing the problems of entrepreneurial discovery, the simple and only rationale for policy is given by the case of informational externalities (Rodrik, 2004): 'good' discoveries are expected to result in a proliferation of 'entries' into the new activity. The entry phase – once initial discoveries have been made and led to initial entrepreneurial success – is when a single discovery begins to be translated into a collective phenomenon, so that agglomeration externalities can be realised. This is a positive step for regional evolution towards smart specialisation, but raises an appropriation issue. The entrepreneur who has made a discovery will not be able to capture a significant fraction of the social value of their initial investment. Consequently, there is a risk that an insufficient number of agents and organisations will invest in this particular type of discovery. So, according to Rodrik, the correction of imperfect appropriation is the main policy problem. While correction mechanisms (such as patents with a broad scope) address the appropriation problem, they block imitative entry, which, to a certain extent, is desirable because entries will translate a single discovery into a collective phenomenon so that agglomeration externalities can be realised. In other words, there is tension between the need for entrepreneurs who make discoveries to capture private returns and the need to prevent this appropriation from foreclosing all the social value of the discovery and this tension causes a problem of incentive alignment.

Aligning incentives through intelligent policy design

Intelligent policy design essentially involves solving the potential conflict between two kinds of incentives that are needed throughout the process: i) incentives to reward those who discover new domains and activities; and ii) incentives to attract other agents and firms and facilitate entries, enabling agglomeration and scale effects to materialise at the next stage. As well demonstrated in Rodrik (2004), these two sets of incentives are not perfectly aligned. To solve this problem, the reward to the entrepreneur who has made a discovery needs to be structured in a way that maximises the spillovers to subsequent entrants and rivals.

What are the mechanisms that will allow the initial discoverer to capture adequate private returns, while not foreclosing the additional social returns resulting from entry? If we think again of the Swiss example of the surgeons and industry suppliers in Basel, it is interesting to see that a mechanism to reward entrepreneurs while maximising spillovers was put in place by the surgeons. The surgeons propagated their vision and their knowledge among the industrialists who then managed to convert their production. They were also sufficiently convincing for the industrialists to transfer their patent to Synthes in exchange for exclusive licences for the commercialisation of products in certain parts of the world. It can truly be said that these surgeons had completely understood the subtle mechanism of rewarding entrepreneurs while maximising spillovers.

Funding experiments and discoveries

Determining the most appropriate method to finance experiments and discoveries as well as the initial development of a new activity is no trivial matter. Here, the uncertainty associated with starting a new activity is coupled with the uncertainty and risks related to the fact that often this activity will be carried out in a region that is little developed. The uncertainty, informational asymmetries and moral hazard[6] are considerable and are likely to permit opportunistic behaviour on the part of entrepreneurs. It will therefore be difficult to attract private investors or even win a share of development funds established by banks as part of their corporate responsibility.

This combination of high uncertainty, asymmetric information and moral hazard, and the fact that R&D typically does not yield results instantaneously, imply a particular funding mechanism: venture capital organisations (VCs). While R&D carried out by small entities and entrepreneurs is often characterised by considerable uncertainty and informational asymmetries, permitting opportunistic behaviour by entrepreneurs, VCs employ a variety of mechanisms to address these information problems. Historical circumstances and structural changes in the organisation of innovation have led to VCs emerging as the dominant form of equity financing for privately held technology-intensive businesses (Hall and Lerner, 2010). At the same time, there are reasons to believe that despite the presence of private VC funds, there might still be a role for public VC programmes in the difficult kinds of contexts described above.

There are several arguments for public investment (Lerner, 1999):

- The structure of venture investments may make them inappropriate for many projects: venture funds tend to make quite substantial investments, even in young firms, and so VC organisations are unwilling to invest in projects that require only small capital infusions.
- The VC industry is limited: VCs back only a tiny fraction of technology-oriented businesses and VC funds are highly geographically concentrated.
- If public VC awards could certify that projects are of high quality, some of the information problems could be overcome and investors could confidently invest in these firms.
- Finally, public finance theory emphasises that subsidies are an appropriate response in the case of activities that generate positive externalities.

These are all valid reasons for public VCs to be complementary to and extensions of private VCs for projects aimed at discovering new areas for future specialisation. Such efforts often have financial requirements that are too small in relation to the average financing scale. The fact that projects may be located in less advanced regions increases the informational problems to such an extent that the usual types of monitoring mechanisms set up by the VCs may seem insufficient or increase the costs too sharply compared to the anticipated profitability. Finally, the essence of entrepreneurial discoveries is the *generation of informational spillovers* (effects of demonstration and emulation) that in themselves represent a rationale for public financing. An important policy tool to examine and develop is therefore a public VC fund; i.e. a public financing mechanism addressing the problems of entrepreneurship and entrepreneurs' projects, given the challenging circumstances of many regional economies (Lerner, 1999).

Capabilities

The information externality raises an important issue and requires the design of mechanisms to subsidise the costs of discoveries. However, the objective of building an economy with an intensive level of entrepreneurial experimentation and discovery requires actions other than simply correcting this market failure.

This is particularly true for regions that are relatively poor in entrepreneurial capabilities. This goal also requires the creation of appropriate conditions for the emergence of multiple microsystems of experiments and discoveries. The performance of entrepreneurs and firms in experimenting with and discovering potential domains for future specialisation may depend upon the way in which they build an external network of connections with universities, laboratories, suppliers and users. The main policy challenge therefore appears to be in facilitating the design of such inter-organisational connections, and the coordination of efforts in the sphere of experimentation and discovery (David and Metcalfe, 2009; Aghion *et al.* 2009). There is plenty of scope for policy to allow firms to create institutions for solving the collective action problems raised by the production and integration of entrepreneurial knowledge and the development of discovery activities (Romer, 1993).[7] The organisational connections may be established explicitly to promote entrepreneurial discovery in the *related variety* framework (see Chapter 2). This is the case of Finnish platforms that have a regional and thematic basis in order to encourage transition, modernisation and diversification dynamics related to existing productive structures (Uotila *et al.* 2012).

In regions that are poor in entrepreneurial capabilities, the main issue is therefore not insufficient incentives (informational externalities) impeding the private effort of the existing entrepreneurs, but the lack of local entrepreneurial knowledge. Policy-makers concerned with this kind of region will face different options for launching a smart specialisation strategy, including the mobilisation of extra-regional resources (see Chapter 4).

Guiding discoveries?

An important policy research issue is the role of policy not only in supporting entrepreneurial discovery but also in influencing the *direction* in which experiments and discoveries should be oriented. Under what conditions can such policy action be undertaken without causing the usual failures of wrong choices and market distortions? In Chapter 2 I set out a typology of structural changes (modernisation, diversification, transition, radical foundation). This typology provides policy-makers with the possibility of thinking ahead and identifying the most desirable structural evolution of the regional economy, given its strengths and weaknesses. The policy-maker can search for the entrepreneurial knowledge and discoveries necessary to realise and validate the policy vision. There is therefore a feedback mechanism from a policy vision – as determined by the identification of structural change that is particularly desirable for the regional economy – to the search for entrepreneurial knowledge in the sectors and institutions corresponding to such a vision. However, subsequent decisions and choices – whether to help and support a particular trend as a potential domain for future specialisation – are determined by the quality of entrepreneurial discoveries that will (or will not) be made.

Box 3.1 The use of technology foresight

The tools grouped under the generic term *technology foresight* (Martin, 2001; Georghiou, 1996) can be very useful. To quote Martin's definition:

> Foresight is the process involved in systematically attempting to look into the longer-term future of science, technology, the economy, the environment and society with the aim of identifying the emerging generic technologies and the underpinning areas of strategic research likely to yield the greatest economic and social benefits.

These tools allow the systematic examination of the technological, economic and social challenges of the large sectors of the regional economy in order to identify the structural changes desired and the technological opportunities that would enable them to be achieved. With regard to these technological opportunities, one interesting idea would be to investigate patenting activities worldwide in the important sectors of the regional economy – what new technology areas do the patenting activities by firms in other regions in the same industry suggest? This is obviously a follower strategy, but it is possible that the activity is new enough for followers not to lag too far behind.

A technology foresight exercise conducted to prepare a regional smart specialisation strategy must be *small-scale* (Aichholzer, 2001), i.e. limited to the development prospects of the important sectors of the regional economy. The regional actors themselves must take charge of it as the government does not have the *ex ante* knowledge regarding what must be done and the collective reflection process triggered by the exercise is just as important as the result (Martin, 2001).

2 Design principle n° 2: inclusiveness and the sleeping giant, excited goblins and hungry dwarfs

Within the regional economy, different sub-systems (sectors, clusters) perform differently. It would be easy to look only at the most dynamic and productive part of the economy to search for entrepreneurial discoveries and select priorities. However, this would represent rather a narrow and exclusive view of smart specialisation. It is also an inefficient process of resource allocation since it is precisely the less dynamic parts of the economy that desperately need structural changes (modernisation, diversification or transition), and therefore need to be part of the smart specialisation strategy. As Phelps (2012) argues:

> While dynamism is crucial, we want dynamism with economic justice – with what I call economic inclusion … It means drawing people into the economic sector of a modern economy, where new ideas for new processes and products are conceived, developed and tested.

Smart specialisation needs to be inclusive. This does not mean that the strategy will support a project in every sector (the last word belongs to entrepreneurial discoveries) but inclusive smart specialisation means giving every sector a chance to be present in the strategy thanks to a good project.

A thought experiment

Let's assume that the regional economy includes a large agrofood sector characterised by weak to moderate innovation capacities, a high-tech cluster and a population of low-tech SMEs operating as subcontractors for the automotive sector, which is based in other regions. Such a structure would be described as involving *a sleeping giant, some excited goblins and a few hungry dwarfs*. Policy-makers should try to prevent the *excited goblins* from cornering all the funding. However, this will inevitably happen as a result of a wait-and-see strategy with policy-makers limiting themselves to observing and detecting entrepreneurial discoveries. The result is presented graphically in Figure 3.1, showing a very narrow view of smart specialisation.

A simple wait-and-see policy would result in seeing the *excited goblins* capture all the priorities. However, the smart specialisation strategy needs to be inclusive (see Figure 3.2) in order to be efficient: the *sleeping giant*, as well as the *hungry dwarfs*, badly need structural changes – modernisation or diversification – and this will happen through a smart specialisation strategy that involves them. However, good projects are likely to be more difficult to

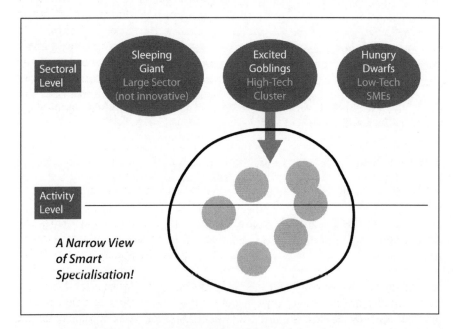

Figure 3.1 An exclusive smart specialisation strategy

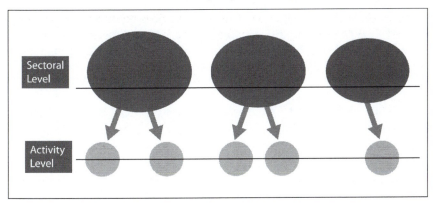

Figure 3.2 An inclusive smart specialisation strategy

identify than in the high-tech cluster context. Yet, if *ex ante* actions are carried out well to support the formation of entrepreneurial knowledge and capabilities, an inclusive strategy will produce results enabling strong entrepreneurial discovery projects to be developed in all parts of the economy.

The beauty of the concept is that a smart specialisation strategy allows policy to be both focused and inclusive. However, the implications of an inclusive strategy are important in terms of the practical implementation of this strategy: some *ex ante* programmes are useful in supporting capability formation and helping entrepreneurial discoveries and emerging activities in sectors where these new activities are desperately needed but difficult to develop spontaneously. In Chapter 5 I will argue that inclusiveness will imply different paces and tempos of the policy because identifying and prioritising good projects in the less dynamic parts of the economy will be more difficult and more costly than in the most dynamic parts. Being inclusive does not mean spreading the money around (or 'everybody will get something') but seeking strong projects throughout the economy.[8]

3 Design principle n° 3: evolving prioritisation

While at *t0* some priorities emerge and subsequent activities will be supported, it is expected that 4–6 years later other discoveries will be made in other parts of the regional system and the subsequent emerging activities will also be supported. This implies that the now 'old' priorities should no longer be part of the smart specialisation strategy. Rodrik (2004) suggests the design of a sunset clause for withdrawing support after an appropriate period of time so that new priorities can be funded. The rationale is simple: after 4–5 years, new activities are no longer new. Whether they have failed or whether they have successfully reached maturity, they should no longer be a priority for the smart specialisation strategy.

Smart specialisation entails strategic and specialised diversification. This principle is important to help policy-makers make choices and decide priorities. These choices are not so difficult since activities not currently selected still retain a chance of being supported in the future.

In the policy dilemma section below, I will deal with the related problem of activities that have been successful as smart specialisation but are no longer new and as such should be removed from the strategy after a certain period of time.

A note on the relationship between smart specialization and competition policy

This principle of funding the generation of new options and not subsidising existing assets in the long term is an essential principle that theoreticians of the so-called *new industrial policy* never fail to invoke. By applying this principle rigorously, innovation policy and competition policy are harmonised, which was not necessarily true in the case of clusters supported for long periods of time through public financing: these long-term subsidies are no longer justified from the innovation policy point of view and are becoming dubious in the eyes of the institutions responsible for competition policies (European Commission, 2012b).

4 Design principle n° 4: observation and evaluation

Observation and information

Fine-grained observation and detection capabilities on the part of policy-makers are becoming critical conditions for the success of a smart specialisation strategy. Fine-grained observation of emerging activities is tremendously important. This is the right level at which to observe the pieces of the knowledge economy that a region can take as basis for smart specialisation. Policy-makers need to differentiate between 'simple' innovation and discoveries that have the potential to spawn new areas of specialisation and might constitute the cornerstone of a smart specialisation strategy. Of course, if the *conceptual* difference between innovation and entrepreneurial discovery is clear (see above), *in practice* the boundaries are blurred, which makes it difficult for policy-makers to detect the 'discoveries' (as opposed to the 'innovations').[9]

Given the immensity of the observation tasks, new models of incentives for encouraging firms to elicit information and bring their own knowledge to the regional policy-maker need to be designed and tested. Such models involve transforming the approach to detect entrepreneurial discoveries from one of 'what does the policy-maker know and how can they find out what they do not know' to one of 'how those who know, the entrepreneurs, can be induced to come forward with that knowledge'.

Ex ante *and* ex post *evaluation*

In his paper Rodrik (2004) emphasised the experimental nature of this type of policy process and concluded that rigorous benchmarking and assessment were central elements: it is the nature of entrepreneurial discovery that not all investments in new activities will pay off. Evaluation is therefore a central policy task so that the support of a particular line of capability formation will not be discontinued too early nor continued so long that subsidies are wasted on non-viable projects.

The point is not to reduce the risk of mistakes, Rodrik (2004) writes, which would result in no discovery at all, but to minimise the costs of mistakes when they do occur by conducting strict assessment procedures both *ex ante*, to evaluate potentials and select priorities, and *ex post*, to identify success and failures.

The precise *ex ante* estimation of the future value of an R&D specialisation that would be required for a cost-benefit analysis is an almost impossible task and one better left to investment markets. As explained below in the section on policy dilemmas, the 'blind giant' metaphor suggests that it is always difficult to assess the stability and sustainability of a specialisation at an early stage.

Some activities show potential – they are new, aimed at experimenting with and discovering technological and market opportunities, and have the potential to provide learning spillovers to others in the economy. They are also characterised by scale and agglomeration economies or coordination failures (in case of a problem of strategic complementarities between upstream and downstream investments that cannot be solved spontaneously). These activities are natural candidates for prioritisation. However, such principles are particularly general and identifying new activities as priorities in real life is no small feat. The *ex ante* assessment of discoveries and potentials involves questions such as whether the considered activity is *new*; whether it aims at *experimenting with and discovering opportunities* and has the potential to generate valuable *information and learning spillovers*; whether the discovery is likely to initiate a desirable *structural change* (modernisation, diversification) for the region; what are the *funding requirements*; are the key *supply factors* (including human capital) available or accessible; is there a *global demand* and who and where are the *main competitors* (see Box 3.2).

> **Box 3.2 Nine *ex ante* criteria to assess projects or domains and select priorities**
>
> 1 Proximity to market: the centre of gravity of smart specialisation strategies is firms and the development of commercial applications; this first criteria is aimed at avoiding projects that would only emphasise fundamental research and/or research infrastructure.

2   Does the activity open a new domain potentially rich in innovation and spillovers? This is the essence of discoveries (versus innovation), namely opening a new domain in which innovations and spillovers will occur.

3   What is the degree of collaboration, and the number of partners involved? The project needs to involve a sufficiently large number of actors. Each new activity set as a priority is a collective experiment.

4   Is public funding needed? Projects that are so promising (in terms of expected private profitability) that they will be undertaken in any case should be rejected (and are probably not true 'discovery projects').

5   What is the significance of the activity for the regional economy? Some excellent projects might be too narrow with regard to their regional significance in terms of job, number of firms, etc. To misquote Nobel Prize winner Robert Solow: we want to see the effect of the strategy in the statistics.

6   What is the capacity of the region to keep the successful activity on its territory, so as to avoid the 'innovation here, benefits elsewhere' syndrome? In general, successful new activities that are related to (and built on) the local innovation ecosystem are easier to keep in the region, while activities created from scratch are more likely to move out of the region.

7   Can this activity realistically drive the region towards a leadership position in the selected niche?

8   What is the degree of connectedness of the activity vis-à-vis the rest of the regional economy? R&D domains with a greater degree of connectedness are more likely to generate spillovers to the connected parts of the economy and create opportunities for structural transformations and evolution than a more isolated domain. To borrow the well-known analogy of Haussmann and Rodrik (2003), it is always good to be in the dense part of the forest so that you can easily jump from one tree to another rather than in a sparsely planted part where it is difficult to move between the trees.

9   Finally, private firms are ready to submit themselves to some kind of monitoring and performance audits.

The use of clear benchmarks and criteria for success and failures in *ex post* assessment also represents a key issue, which might influence the ability of the policy-maker to detect and correct mistakes sufficiently early. *Ex post* assessment is, however, difficult. As Rodrik (2013b) says so well, it is not because, in many contexts (such as smart specialisation policies), application of the most rigorous and academically recognised methods is not possible that all attempts at assessment should be abandoned. We must at least establish *ex ante* cost, productivity, employment and innovation objectives, the fulfilment of which can subsequently be verified. Furthermore, this must be done while also taking into account the changes and turbulence that can characterise the project's environment during the five or six years of its prioritisation.

5 Design principle n° 5: support of early stage and growth of new activities

Beyond entrepreneurial discovery and the choice of priorities, the initial growth of the new activity is going to encounter familiar obstacles, coordination problems between necessary investments at different key points of the emerging microsystem (equipment, specialised services, etc.) and supply problems of public goods specific to the new activity (training, research, etc.). All these problems were brilliantly resolved by the Basel surgeons and are generally well dealt with in countries and regions with a strong tradition of private institutions as a solution to problems of coordination and specific public goods (Weder and Grubel, 1993). Generally however public policies and interventions are necessary.

Most projects with the potential to spawn new activities require simultaneous large-scale investments to be made in order to become profitable. All the necessary services and complementary activities have fixed costs and can only start if the potential provider has sufficient positive expectations regarding the future of the smart specialisation strategy. There are various solutions to such coordination problems, which are not necessarily based on subsidisation (see Rodrik, 2004). Resolving coordination failures also involves responding to the new *knowledge needs* of traditional industries that are starting to adapt and apply a general purpose technology. This entails the provision of adequate supply responses (in human capital formation), by subsidising the follower region's access to problem-solving expertise from researchers in the leader region, and by ensuring the development of local expertise to sustain the incremental improvement, as well as the maintenance of specialised application technologies in the region.[10]

6 Back to Region X

Let us return to Region X that I presented in the previous chapter (Figure 2.2 and Figure 2.3). I have just described a few policy designs that were applied in Region X and resulted in the identification of three priorities:

- reliance on entrepreneurial discoveries (including the formation and structuring of entrepreneurial knowledge);
- inclusive strategy (projects and activities are not only coming from the excited 'photonics guys' but also from the *sleeping giant* – breeding – and the *hungry dwarfs* – ceramics); and
- *ex ante* assessment and selection.

The other two design principles (regarding evolving prioritisation and early growth support) will be applied later as the strategy is developed over time.

With these design principles, inefficiencies and distortions are minimised because of the relationships of these new activities with existing structures (thus the increasing likelihood of spillovers towards connected domains); because of the inclusive nature of the policy (some traditional sectors are involved); because of the fact that after a couple of years these activities will be removed from the smart specialisation strategy; and because a strong evaluation process will be organised. Inefficiencies and distortions would have occurred if, for example, the region had decided to create a cancer research institute or a nanoscience lab with no obvious connection to any productive or research structures in the region.

Of course it remains to be seen how these activities will grow, how they will transform the structures, how important the spillovers will be in supporting the entry and agglomeration of similar and complementary competences and assets, and finally, how new priorities will be set later through a continuous process of entrepreneurial discoveries and experiments that are supported throughout the system.

On policy complementarities

Our emphasis on entrepreneurial discovery helps to show that there is no contradiction between a smart specialisation strategy and the now fashionable policy for start-ups and young technological enterprises (Veugelers, 2009). On the contrary, smart specialisation needs the other policy, unless the required density of entrepreneurial experiments and discoveries is not produced, in which case smart specialisation will fail owing to a deficit of entrepreneurial information about future priorities.

It is also clear that there is no contradiction between smart specialisation and the whole set of horizontal policies. The latter is critical, *ex ante*, to ensure good framework conditions to propel entrepreneurial discovery. It is also critical, *ex post*, as the initial new prioritised activities have reached some degree of maturity and will find better-adapted supports through horizontal policy instruments and are no longer within the smart specialisation strategy.

7 Policy dilemmas

The concept of smart specialisation strategy brings into increasingly sharp relief three innovation policy dilemmas that are present to some degree in any innovation policy. The formulation of these dilemmas forms the basis of the last part of this chapter, to be developed further in Chapter 5, which deals with more practical issues concerning policy design and implementation.

The space for smart specialisation

What is the right space for the deployment of a smart specialisation strategy? Is it the administrative space of a region, or the space in which the relevant resources are available and can be deployed? Neither predefined 'regions' nor specific sectors can be used, *ex ante*, to determine the boundaries of smart specialisation dynamics, as explained above.

In particular, regions are open and likewise smart specialisation is not a closed process. There is no such thing as an autarkic, self-sufficient region. Whatever we call it – the knowledge ecology or the industrial commons – the collective R&D, engineering and manufacturing capabilities that sustain innovation are not necessarily deployed and contained within strict regional boundaries (Amin and Cohendet, 2004). Their development is likely to defy administrative frontiers. In other words, resources in the knowledge economy are not immobile and specific to each region. Extra-regional entrepreneurship, like extra-regional finance and skilled business services, can initiate and continue new activities in regions where those factors of production are scarce. By the same token, such extra-regional resources (including research services) can develop and expand the capacity of small regional enterprises launched by local entrepreneurs. This raises the question of the larger ecology of innovation to which the particular regional system belongs.

Migration and the role of extra-regional resources

I have to acknowledge that in many cases the relationship between existing regional productive assets and the entrepreneurial discovery and subsequent developments is weak. In such cases the stimulus and dynamism are likely to be driven from outside. They do not come from endogenous capabilities as in the cases of Morez, Lyon, Finland and Basel (see Chapter 2). The entrepreneurial discovery takes the form of a 'migration' of extra-regional resources that will combine with existing assets to open up a new domain of opportunities. However, the existing assets in the considered region must be sufficiently developed for their combination with extra-regional resources to permit the initiation of local learning processes and capacity construction dynamics. A case in point is Region Y with an important tourism activity. However, the development of information and communications technology (ICT) applications to transform some segments of the sector will come from another region. This development can become a smart specialisation for Region Y if, and only if, it will generate local spillovers and the formation of capabilities so that R&D and innovation activity will be developed in the region. Otherwise, because of the weak relationship, the tourism sector will be improved (through the ICT development), which is a good thing, but no new capabilities will be built within the regional economy.

The time for smart specialisation

Policy-makers who are willing to influence the process through which the regional economy will develop some new specialisations will face a particular type of the so-called Blind Giant's Quandary, meaning that public agencies have the greatest opportunity to influence future growth trajectory during a time when they know least about what should be done (David, 2005). There is thus a need to identify (and act during) the windows of opportunity in which interventions may amplify virtuous developments. However, on the other hand the identification of activities to be prioritised requires that evaluation and subsequent decisions (support) should happen at a certain point in the development cycle where degrees of local commitment and development have already occurred (in order to avoid the 'lottery of the early stages').

Changing priorities and policy continuity

According to principle n°3, priorities are not selected forever. The goal is to diversify the system through the generation of new options. It is therefore crucial to regularly revisit the portfolio of prioritised activities. After a certain period of time, the 'old' priorities funded under the smart specialisation strategy should be withdrawn from the strategy so that 'new' priorities can be supported (in a context of limited public budget).

Nevertheless, emergence and early growth do require time. The support of new activities needs some kind of continuity in funding R&D and other innovation-related activities. This dilemma is, however, not as severe as it might appear at first glance. Changing priorities do not mean that the 'old' activity will no longer find funding to finance its R&D and innovation activities. Rather, it will just move from the smart specialisation instrument to the horizontal innovation policy that provides other funding instruments in a non-preferential way. In that sense, the smart specialisation strategy and horizontal instruments require strong complementarity within the framework of the general regional innovation policy.

8 Summary of Chapter 3

This chapter comprised a detailed analysis of the five design principles that enable the problems posed by the conception and implementation of the strategy to be resolved: entrepreneurial discovery and level of aggregation; the inclusive nature of the strategy; the evolving nature of the strategy; evaluation; and facilitation of the first phases of growth. Three dilemmas – concerning the timing and space of the strategy and the continuity of financing – are discussed in conclusion.

Notes

1 In Chapter 4 I will discuss the value of more sophisticated taxonomies to design a smart specialisation strategy.
2 Some parts of this chapter draw on Foray and Rainoldi (2013).
3 See Rodrik (2004) as well as Metcalfe (1995, 2014) for a similar argument. According to Metcalfe (2014: p. 29): 'The case for market does not of course imply that governments have no role to play. Quite the contrary, whether in respect of the regulation of the market process or in respect of the fostering business

experimentation the state and the market constitute complementary aspects of a mixed system.'

4 Unlike Aghion (2012) and Aghion *et al.* (2011), I do not want to confuse industrial policy with sectoral policy. If there is any *new* industrial policy agenda, it should not be expressed in sectoral terms, but rather at the mid-grained granularity level of *new activities* where potential failures are not so costly and many opportunities may be identified.

5 It is interesting to observe that this level of *activity* does not appear in the typology of government policies for innovation and entrepreneurship of Chatterji *et al.* (2013) that distinguishes the general level of the economy (horizontal policy), the sector level (vertical policy) and the firm level (policy that may be either horizontal or vertical). Now the validity of the new industrial policy approaches – those that want to generate new specialities while preserving decentralised entrepreneurial dynamics; those that also want to provide each region with opportunities for action – are essentially based on this mid-grained level of granularity. However, it must be said that the authors mainly study existing and therefore relatively traditional policies.

6 The term 'moral hazard' refers to inefficient behaviour on the part of one actor in a transaction caused by differences in information available to parties to the transaction. Regarding applications in finance and innovation, see Hall and Lerner (2010).

7 Kelley and Arora (1996) provide interesting examples of dedicated programmes in the USA (for example, the *Manufacturing Technology Center*) aimed at promoting inter-firm learning and connections between technology developers and potential users. These cases provide an illustration of how industrial policy can support and promote collective actions by SMEs to explore new technological and market opportunities.

8 The European Commission has produced a short cartoon devoted to smart specialisation strategy in which the scenario is based on this trilogy – *sleeping giant, excited goblins* and *hungry dwarfs*. The film can be viewed via the following link: http://ec.europa.eu/regional_policy/videos/video-details.cfm?LAN=EN&vid=1342.

9 See Chapter 4 for suggestions on measuring entrepreneurial discovery.

10 The connection between R&D projects in less advanced regions and research teams and institutions in a leader region that can provide problem-solving expertise is one of the goals of the so-called *teaming and twinning* policy instruments prepared in the framework of the Horizon 2020 programme of the European Union. These instruments are relevant for building and developing different kinds of partnerships between regional research entities and leading international counterparts. As such, the design and objectives of these instruments are perfectly aligned with the knowledge and competence needs of smart specialisation strategies in peripheral regions.

4 Goal variations according to regional development

The goals of a smart specialisation strategy have already been mentioned. However, what was covered in Chapter 3 will enable us to clarify those goals even further. This chapter will summarise the goals of smart specialisation strategies and I will then question the pertinence of these objectives according to the development levels of the regions, as well as with regard to questions of interregional coordination within a 'superior' entity (such as the European Union – EU).[1]

1 A summary of the goals

It is now possible to identify the precise goals of smart specialisation and propose how to quantify progress towards attaining them. The principles that form the baseline of the policy process make it similar to the agenda of the so-called *new industrial policy*. The following themes:

- a *non-neutral* policy;
- keeping market forces working (*entrepreneurial discovery* as the main informational input);
- an *interactive process* between policy and the private sector;
- *activity* (not sectors or individuals) as the right level of intervention;
- *evolving* priorities;
- the *experimental* nature of policy
- what is important here is the *process* that helps reveal areas of desirable interventions

compose the frame of reference. From this perspective a smart specialisation strategy is just a good economic policy of the type that attempts to make two critical, and somewhat conflicting, requirements compatible: identifying priorities in a vertical logic and keeping market forces working to reveal domains and areas where priorities should be selected. From this it follows that the main objectives of a smart specialisation policy are not about generating technological uniformity and monoculture, nor about prioritising sectors or narrowing down the development path of a regional economy. On the contrary, smart specialisation goals involve:

- facilitating the emergence and early growth of new activities that are potentially rich in innovation and spillovers;
- diversifying regional systems through the generation of new options; and
- generating critical mass, critical networks, and critical clusters within a diversified system.

Smart specialisation versus high-tech policy and cluster policy

Smart specialisation as a regional strategy conveys the message quite strongly that the best future for many regions is not necessarily to be found within the high-tech industry. A valuable strategy is to start from the existing sectoral structures and thence derive a portfolio of strategic options. Of course, high-tech R&D and innovation will be present everywhere, but in many cases more as a way to modernise or diversify old traditional industries than as a production objective *per se*. In view of the policy design and goals, it becomes increasingly clear that a smart specialisation policy should not be reduced to a high-tech policy. R&D and innovation-related activities are relevant and important in any sector of the economy.

Furthemore, we should not confuse a smart specialisation policy with a cluster policy. I have already discussed cluster policies in Chapter 1: cluster policies not driven by a smart specialisation process are vulnerable to risks caused by the difficulty of assessing claimed potential and the corresponding risk of endorsing 'hopes' rather than 'actualities'. Of course, generating a vibrant, innovative cluster is a desirable (and logical) outcome of a smart specialisation strategy and, arguably, an 'emergent property' of a smart specialisation process (see the examples in Chapter 2, which all involved some kind of agglomeration and clustering phases). However, a cluster policy designed in a top-down way – i.e. very much influenced by traditional industrial policies – does not fundamentally change and is even likely to accentuate strongly mimetic programmes of local and national industrial development. Such top-down policy processes of cluster creation result in the fostering of knowledge base homogenisation, wasteful duplication and the dissipation of potential agglomeration economies at system level, as a multiplicity of imitative local government authorities compete to attract the small finite pool of mobile capital and management and knowledge resources. The resulting duplication, unproductive uniformity and lack of imagination and vision in setting R&D and cluster priorities can be expected to produce poor results at system level (the EU for instance), with most regions remaining unattractive and unable to compete with other territories to capture high-value assets and retain their best resources. Smart specialisation, on the other hand, involves the fundamental process of discovering what makes a local knowledge base original and distinctive, thereby driving the formation of capabilities and clusters that are likely to be unique in the type of knowledge-driven activities they will develop.

As clearly explained by Bresnahan *et al.* (2002), the questions about the origin of a cluster and its growth are actually different and the forces underlying the emergence of an industrial cluster differ from those needed to ensure its continued growth. Network effect, agglomeration economies, knowledge spillovers – in short, the increasing returns framework – are what count when studying the growth of a cluster after it has taken off. However, it is difficult to get that new cluster started and what is a challenge for researchers is to understand these initial conditions, the so-called *genetic causal moment*. At that stage, 'old economy' factors are crucial and these involve firms' building capabilities, managerial skills, supply of skilled labour, and connection to markets. In other words, according to Bresnahan *et al.* (2002), starting a cluster entails:

- building the economic foundations for an industry or a technology, which includes the importance of being linked to a sizeable and growing demand and the availability of a proper supply of key factors; and
- finding the spark of entrepreneurship to get it going.

Smart specialisation, as is now clear, is about the *genetic causal moment*: the spark of entrepreneurship (entrepreneurial discovery) that is likely to generate strong informational spillovers to redirect the productive decisions of others (entries and agglomerations). Of course, when the development of the new speciality has been initiated (entrepreneurial discovery and early growth) and an agglomeration and concentration dynamic is triggered, a cluster policy – understood as a tool though which to internalise local externalities and improve the competitiveness of the now-existing cluster – becomes fully relevant (Ketels, 2013).

As Rodriguez-Clare (2005) rightly says, policies to promote entrepreneurial discoveries and cluster policies are complementary. They must be combined and a particular combination will correspond to each country. I also think that these policies must be activated during the different stages of the smart specialisation cycle, with entrepreneurial discovery policies as the departure point of this cycle.

Metrics

The goals of smart specialisation policy identified above suggest natural metrics for measuring progress. Clearly, the measurement aspect of the smart specialisation agenda is still in progress. The indicators for the above-mentioned goals will have to be somewhat eclectic since the trends and evolutions underlying the *fundamental logic of the development of new specialities* are not captured by the standard knowledge and innovation indicator framework.

From the start we have specified the meaning of 'specialisation' in the smart specialisation language. Smart specialisation does not refer to the fact that a region is specialised relative to other regions in a passive sense, but to the development of new activities and specialities based on regional concentration of resources and competences. Thus, the existing indicator framework that provides specialisation metrics and thus profiles of regions – while very useful for a wide range of assessment purposes – does not capture the localisation and concentration of activities.[2]

However, the need for data and indicators concerning smart specialisation is critical. Without metrics and indicators, as well as regular data collection, the patterns of smart specialisation strategies will not be discernible and policy-makers will be unable to track progress, assess structural transformations and compare strategies. There is therefore a pressing need for further research and development in this area to build a collection of statistics on several dimensions of smart specialisation and produce new ways of measuring emerging trends regarding entrepreneurial discoveries, the development of new activities, diversification of the system and the generation of critical clusters; in other words, measuring progress towards the different goals of smart specialisation. This effort is essential if the economics of smart specialisation is to progress beyond the purely abstract, and allow theory to be linked to practice. Within the framework of this book, I will restrict myself to a few key suggestions for further development.

Measuring entrepreneurial discovery

The measurement of entrepreneurial discoveries will constitute the key factor of quantitative approaches aimed at better estimating the vigour of smart specialisation processes and strategies. As has already been discussed, the observation of the phenomenon and the distinction between entrepreneurial discovery and 'simple' innovation are not easy empirical investigation objectives. Progress in measuring the phenomenon could in turn permit a better understanding of what distinguishes these two logics.

The research agenda for designing indicators adapted to the measurement of entrepreneurial discovery in my opinion comprises three sections, which more or less correspond to the classic distinction between input, output and outcome indicators.

First, we can measure how the framework conditions of an innovation system (regional or otherwise) are favourable to entrepreneurial discovery. With this objective in mind, emphasis must be placed especially on the measurements of the relational density and diversity of economic agents within a given area. Indeed, even more so than innovation, entrepreneurial discoveries originate from the connection between economic agents and their diversity (Fleming *et al.* 2007). This is confirmed, for example, by the story of the surgeons and mechanics in the Basel region of Switzerland, or the Lyon silk manufacturers and chemists in France, or the wood pulp manufacturers and nanoscience researchers in Finland.

Second, we can try to measure entrepreneurial discovery processes *ex post*. Here, patent data are obviously of prime importance. It has already been stressed that the very nature of the discovery means that it is clearly not patentable and that the maximisation of spillovers generated by this discovery requires alternative reward mechanisms than patents or other exclusive rights. On the other hand, when firms have entered the new domain and achieve specific developments, the resulting inventions are patented. These patterns will have relatively similar characteristics regarding timing, geographical situation and technological classes. Consequently, it might be thought that the observation of these *related patents* can allow the *ex post* development of entrepreneurial discovery indicators. These related patents reflect nothing more than a multiple-invention phenomenon (Lamb and Easton, 1984) or *positive duplication* (a duplication not resulting from pure imitation but from the simultaneous entry of different inventors into the same new area of invention opportunities)[3] (see Figure 4.1).

Third, we can envisage measuring the structural change – transition, diversification, modernisation and radical foundation – resulting from the entrepreneurial discovery and subsequent development of new activities. Again patent data can be very useful. The transition or modernisation dynamics can be observed via the evolution of the content of inventions within the framework of a given sector. For example, Nikulainen (2008) documents the modernisation of the wood pulp industry in Finland, showing between 1980 and 1995 that the patents of this industry are characterised by inventions in mechanical engineering and process engineering, whereas from 1996 onwards these patents are increasingly characterised by inventions in the electrical engineering domain. As far as the dynamics of the transition of the mechanical engineering industry towards medical technologies are concerned, we can see clearly, thanks to the patent data, the evolution of inventions by Small and Medium-sized Enterprises (SMEs) from one domain to another. The research agenda for the measurement of entrepreneurial discoveries is thus

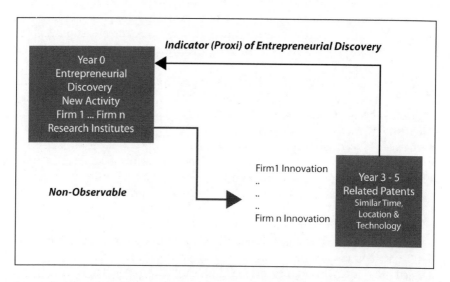

Figure 4.1 Ex post measurement of entrepreneurial discovery

obviously crucial and varied. The research agenda developed by Boschma, Frenken, Neffke and co-authors is central here since its aim is to provide indicators and collect data to measure industrial and structural changes at regional level.

2 The relevance of goals for different types of region

There are as many cases as there are regions in Europe. Each region is specific in terms of history, economic development and its economic and political integration into the EU. There are also particular framework conditions that can be specifically national or regional. Typologies are useful in finding similarities and regularities to allow researchers and policy-makers to deal with a small number of cases in which the issues and challenges involved are somewhat similar. The goal of this book is not to invent a new typology and I would like to maintain the EC classification of regions into three main categories:[4]

- less developed regions (GDP/head less than 75% of the regional average)
- transition regions (GDP/head between 75 and 90% of the regional average)
- more developed regions (GDP/head more than 90% of the regional average)

The smart specialisation policy framework provides strategies and roles for any region. Indeed, the concept is built around the fact that there is not only *one game in town* in terms of R&D and innovation.[5] Indeed there are many other kinds of productive and potentially beneficial activities, apart from the invention of fundamental knowledge, needed for the development of general purpose technologies and tools (GPTs), such as information and communications technology (ICT) or biotechnology.[6] There are in fact different logics or orders of innovation (Bresnahan and Trajtenberg, 1995; Bresnahan, 2010). In other words, innovation often involves the development of applications of a GPT that has been invented elsewhere. Some regions can of course specialise in the invention of the GPT, while others will invest in the 'co-invention' of applications to address particular problems of quality and productivity in one or several important sectors of their economies. First, I am going to explain the particular properties of GPTs that offer each region – regardless of its level of development – certain opportunities to position themselves competitively in the knowledge economy. I will then examine the cases of regions situated at different levels of development.

The GPT framework

Most GPTs play the role of 'enabling technologies', opening up new opportunities rather than offering complete, final solutions. This phenomenon involves what are called *innovational complementarities*, i.e. the productivity of R&D in a user sector increases as a consequence of innovation in the GPT and the very effort of the users themselves to 'co-invent' applications. These complementarities magnify the effects of innovation in the GPT, and help propagate them throughout the economy. These are the peculiar properties of technical change that it is crucial to capture owing to their centrality to explain the complex relationships between the invention of high tech and the dynamics of innovation and productivity in more traditional sectors.

The production of knowledge and technological solutions in user sectors (i.e. the development of new applications) is crucial to ensure the effective diffusion of the GPT. This process is called 'co-invention of application' to stress its creative aspect. Expressed in economists' language, the successive inventions of a GPT extend the frontier of invention possibilities for the whole economy, while application developments change the production function of particular sectors.

The externality structure between the two types of sectors (inventors of the GPT and co-inventors of applications or, more simply, producer and user) is complex but important to grasp thoroughly in order to understand the opportunities and challenges for less advanced regions with mainly traditional industries and services (Bresnahan and Trajtenberg, 1995; Bresnahan 2010).

A first type of externality is known as knowledge spillovers. This is related to the role of GPTs as 'enabling technologies': basic GPT inventions generate new opportunities for developing applications in particular sectors.

A second type of externality is known as market spillovers, which result when the market for the innovation causes some of the benefits thus created to flow to users and not the innovating firm. It is this 'leakage' of benefits through the operation of market forces, rather than the flow of knowledge itself, that distinguishes market spillovers from knowledge spillovers. Any time a GPT inventor creates a new technology, or reduces the cost of producing an existing technology, the natural market forces will tend to cause some of the benefits thus created to be passed on to users.

The third type, which is also a vertical one, involves feedback from the development of new applications: application inventions increase the size of the market for ICT, improving the economic return to ICT invention.

The fourth type of externality is a horizontal one that occurs among users: the early user's experience lowers the later user's cost of co-invention and adoption. This type of externality (also called increasing return to adoption) creates an incentive to wait.

The complementarities between GPT inventions and the co-inventions of applications – characterised by this complicated externality structure – inject a dynamic feedback loop in which advances in the GPT lead to unpredictable inventions in applications, which in turn raise the return to further GPT inventions. The externality structure also creates a lot of inertia in the system (David and Wright, 1999): when events evolve favourably, a long-term dynamic of technological change develops, consisting of large-scale investments in research and innovation whose social and private marginal rates of return attain high levels. In the opposite case, the GPT system (including producers and users) is likely to be trapped in a low level of R&D in both types of sectors. This externality structure logically creates several lags: between invention and first co-invention; between co-invention and further investment in the basic invention; and between early co-invention and the generalisation of co-invented ideas.

Goal relevance for less developed and transition regions and the GPT framework

Goal relevance for these kinds of regions is clear as the graphical representations in Chapter 2 show. Horizontal policies, although necessary, are not sufficient, and there is a need for resource concentration and prioritisation to fill the gap in a few domains and generate spillovers and growth that will tend to affect the whole economy. However, one question remains open. Are there enough technological opportunities for all regions? A question I have asked from the beginning of this book. Here the GPT framework is important.

Co-inventions *as opportunity to act in the knowledge economy play*

Co-invention is an important notion here (Bresnahan, 2003). The very act of adopting ICTs (or any other GPTs) to improve operational efficiency or product quality in a given sector of industry or service is by no means a simple task. ICT applications are not ready and waiting on the shelf for new users. The co-invention of applications involves a great deal of R&D, design and redesign, i.e. a collection of knowledge-driven activities. Smart specialisation strategy therefore implies rejecting the principle of a sharp division of labour between knowledge producers and knowledge users. All regions face challenges in terms of improving operational efficiency and product quality in their businesses and industries and making these improvements is often a matter of R&D, capability development and innovation.

For many regions, the complex structure of a GPT trajectory (which is distributed among fundamental inventors and application developers) is an opportunity to be 'in the game': the development of biotechnology applications for fisheries, ICT applications for tourism, and nanotechnology applications for the agrofood or pulp and paper industry are strongly knowledge-driven activities through which a less developed region or a transition region can build capabilities in a new R&D domain and modernise and transform important sectors. The intersection between the potential of a GPT application and an important sector of the regional economy defines the feasibility space for a smart specialisation strategy, i.e. the space where entrepreneurial experiments are expected to produce socially useful knowledge concerning possible paths of structural change.

The smart specialisation strategy seeks to avoid hindering relative positions between followers and leaders with the less advanced regions being locked into the development of applications and incremental innovations. Of course, smart specialisation does not have magical properties to transform laggards into global leaders. However, at the very least, a smart specialisation strategy transforms less advanced regions into *good followers*: a region in transition that is building capabilities and agglomerating knowledge resources in a certain domain of application, enabling it to capture knowledge spillovers from the leaders (those inventing the basic technology), attracts further knowledge assets and develops an ecosystem of innovation with the prospect and realistic hope of becoming a leader. A leader? Yes, but a leader not in inventing the generic technology but in co-inventing specific applications (for example, ICTs used in logistics or biotechnology applications for monitoring agricultural production).

This means that the follower regions and the firms within them, by designing and implementing a smart specialisation strategy, become part of a more realistic and practicable competitive environment – defining an arena of competition in which the players (other regions with similar strategies) are more symmetrically endowed, and a viable market niche can be created that will not be quickly eroded by the entry of larger external competitors. This means that smart specialisation is definitely not only for the best regions; just the opposite. It is a unique stairway to excellence for less developed and transition regions.

The Knowledge and Excellence in European Nanotechnology (KEEN) Regions project shows clearly that there are opportunities for any region in the knowledge economy – for the leading regions in the fundamental invention of a GPT (Grenoble, France, and Flanders, Belgium) as well as other regions that are strong in developing applications for their manufacturing activities (Veneto, Italy, and the Basque Country, Spain). With KEEN as a mechanism to maximise interactions and knowledge flows between these two categories of regions, a high rate of innovation and vigorous dynamics are expected in all regions based on the exploitation of the many positive externalities that characterise technological change in the GPT framework (see above).

What about the peripheral regions?

The most peripheral and less advanced regions will be in difficulty when it comes to developing a smart specialisation strategy. The lack of entrepreneurial capacities and the weakness of administrative capacities will combine to make this process uncertain and almost impossible. However, it cannot be disputed that these regions, more so than others, need structural transformations and diversification of their economy. New activities focusing on the modernisation of traditional sectors, the transition or diversification of certain sectors towards new markets and perhaps the radical founding of high-productivity industrial domains are absolutely necessary. The question is therefore not to know *whether* structural change is necessary, but rather *how to go about it?* Does a smart specialisation policy constitute an appropriate, feasible and effective approach for this type of region?

Some authors give a distinctly negative answer: it is better to give up the idea of trying to develop new specialities based on entrepreneurial discovery and local resource concentration mechanisms since that has never worked and instead we must give priority to connecting these regions to external knowledge reservoirs. This is the idea of 'clusters versus pipelines' defended by Rodriguez-Pose and Dahl Fitjar (2013): 'the promotion of local interaction in what may be relatively small and/or remote areas may not yield the expected results and is likely to be unable to undermine trends towards the concentration of economic activity in core areas'. These authors therefore disqualify what they call 'the buzz option', i.e. all those policies that have favoured the local concentration of resources in the theoretical context of local innovation systems. They argue that the buzz option has demonstrated a 'limited capacity to dynamise the economy and to generate sustainable development in intermediate and peripheral areas'. These authors prefer the so-called pipeline option. This involves promoting interaction at a distance and this implies building bridges or pipelines from the local economy to the outside world.

The mobilisation of external resources is obviously a good idea and the logic of the smart specialisation policy certainly does not reject it. As already stated (see Chapter 3), there is no such thing as an autarkic, self-sufficient region. Connections and pipelines are thus part of the panoply of instruments allowing the initiation and support of new activities in a particular region.[7]

However, the idea of local concentration of resources and skills remains valid and fundamental if we want there to be a receiver at the end of the pipeline. This is the absorption capacity theory. As emphasised in the section devoted to the scale, scope and spillover rationale (Chapter 2), even the ability to capture knowledge spillovers generated by others depends on the existence of a sufficiently large R&D sector in close proximity (Trajtenberg, 2002).

In other words, the pipeline option corresponds to an external resource mobilisation logic that is absolutely in phase with smart specialisation policy. However, it cannot be a self-standing strategy inasmuch as internal capacities must be built and a certain polarisation created (the role of smart specialisation) to take advantage of it.

Thus, I suggest that 'clusters versus pipeline' is not a debate. These options are complementary and must be mobilised simultaneously to allow the new speciality to develop. In any case, to reiterate the reflections of Rodriguez-Clare (2005), neither of them can replace entrepreneurial discovery policies that should always come first. Hence, Figure 4.2 presents the different policies and options within the context of a smart specialisation strategy of a less developed region.

Virtues of a big-push type policy?

When entrepreneurial capacities are weak – nonexistent even – it will be difficult to create the new activities that will be the source of future

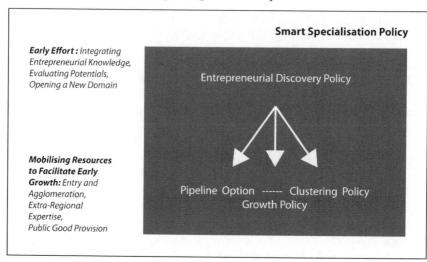

Figure 4.2 Smart specialisation policy in peripheral regions

specialities and structural transformation of the economy. We are therefore confronted with something similar to a development economics problem – less so with regard to the production of basic infrastructures (human capital and institutions as fundamentals of growth) than with regard to industrial policy aimed at diversifying the system.[8] For this purpose, mechanisms aimed at mobilising external resources – diaspora, cooperation network, inter-regional association – are important, as is a policy of the big-push type. It must be clearly understood that a big-push type policy (Rosenstein-Rodan, 1961; Murphy *et al.* 1989) cannot be restricted to mega-investment in science and technology, which is likely to turn into a white elephant – if complementary investments are not carried out with a view to coordinating the new technological infrastructure with the needs and capacities of firms. If we return to the example of Galicia, the *Campus do Mar* in Vigo, Spain, will only be able to trigger the development of new specialities to transform traditional sectors (fisheries and canning) if a sufficient number of firms in these sectors link up with the new university to collectively develop innovative solutions for the modernisation and diversification of the sectors concerned. In other words, the establishment of the knowledge infrastructure must be completed through the organisation of coordination between the latter and industry. This coordination can take the form of programmes to improve the absorption and learning capacities of firms in the sector or plans for supporting the creation of firms specialised in the development of technological solutions at the interface between campus and industry. I am talking here about well-known problems – knowledge and technology transfers. However, what makes the question specific is that the success of this transferability is crucial, since it is the sole justification and economic rationality for the big push (i.e. the infrastructure's investment).

The value of smart specialisation strategy for leading regions

More than innovation, entrepreneurial discovery is what facilitates evolution and changes in regional or national systems of innovation. Even the most advanced systems need exploration, experimentation and the discovery of new domains beyond the current routines of innovation. This is true for systems entering a period of decline and obsolescence, as well as for those that currently show strong performances. In leading regions too, entrepreneurial knowledge and discovery aimed at opening new domains beyond current routines need to be detected, supported and prioritised.

Perhaps the best regions or countries have super-efficient systems in which discoveries are made continuously and good framework conditions enable new activities to grow well so that strategic diversification is happening continuously. Silicon Valley, USA, for example, is well equipped to catch the new waves of opportunity because of its innovation climate. The climate there seems to be good at incubating not only ICT start-ups but is favouring the continuous development of new specialities such as the most recent wave of green technologies. However, in most successful regions, the success of today is not a guarantee of success for tomorrow. Successful clusters are not protected against the disease of 'routinised' innovation efforts (Baumol, 2002), creative myopia and collective inertia. Many historical cases tell the same story of successful clusters or regions not capable of reinventing themselves when new waves of technologies and market opportunities arrive. Collections of resources can turn into *communities of inertia*; in other words, communities in which the persistence of behaviours, values and beliefs that had previously worked well predominates. Firms may even tend to respond to the new challenge by placing even more confidence in the organisational routines of the past, a phenomenon that Sull (2001) designated as 'active inertias'. As this author clearly demonstrates, tyre companies in the Akron region of the USA responded to the technological challenge posed by Michelin (France) by striving to improve incrementally their own technology that had become obsolete and heavily investing in new production capacities without making any radical technological changes to them. Akron was wiped off the map.

Moreover, when innovation is concentrated in a single large firm, it is proven that such a firm and its employees suffer from creative myopia. They are not inclined to look outside, to learn from others (Agrawal *et al.* 2010).

Thus, a relevant question for these leading regions is the following: are there enough experiments and discoveries beyond the current innovative routines? In leading regions too, entrepreneurs exploring new domains beyond and outside the innovation routines need to be identified and supported.

3 The goals of smart specialisation strategies in relation to coordination needs at European level

I have already stressed that the political salience of smart specialisation is also the result of its potential contributions to greater efficiencies in resource allocation (human capital, research infrastructures, specialised services for innovation) at system level (for example the level of an integrated regional system such as the EU). Smart specialisation offers a policy process for local strategies based on identifying and developing original, distinctive and fertile areas of specialisation for the future that are likely to *promote greater diversity* in the areas of knowledge and expertise within the system (i.e. the EU), thereby:

- rendering each regional economy more able to acquire some critical mass in key activities and enjoy the benefits of distinct local agglomeration economies; and
- making the whole system more diversified and endowed with more opportunities for internal spillovers and options for future evolutions.

From local decisions to general coordination

There has been some misunderstanding of the concept of smart specialisation that is likely to drive a misuse of it as a policy approach. According to this misunderstanding, smart specialisation is a tool that can be applied to organise a top-down process of prioritisation among countries (i.e. by the EC) or among regions (i.e. by a central government at country level). In such a vision of smart specialisation, the omniscient central planner (either the EC or a national government) has enough information and coordination capabilities to organise the big European (or national) R&D factory. The idealised outcome would be a perfect system of complementarities and coherence that will succeed in eliminating any inefficiency arising from duplication and imitation. This is, of course, a new version of the great fantasy of industrial planners but it is not what smart specialisation is about.

Smart specialisation involving a process of entrepreneurial discovery offers another, less ambitious but more realistic, alternative for general coordination. By definition, regional smart specialisation strategies are going to produce a sort of burgeoning of new activities whose coherence is 'local'. This means that priorities are chosen essentially on the basis of the relationship between the new project (new activity) and the potentials and needs of existing local structures.

As we know, the main informational input in establishing priorities needs to be entrepreneurial knowledge – knowledge that is not only about *science and technology* but is largely made up of *economic* knowledge about markets and competitors, i.e. what will work economically given local and global productive and business opportunities (see Figure 2.1). The decisions made are assumed to take into account competitive environments, global markets and rivals' strategies. In other words, the setting of priorities is driven by the entrepreneurial knowledge and the decisions to explore a new market niche, not by the policy-makers' dream of developing another biotechnology cluster.

The coordination that will result is a soft one that will not avoid all duplications. However, this is the only reasonable way to minimise duplication and improve coordination. In a sense, the smart specialisation idea occupies an intermediate place in the conceptual space of general coordination solutions between the Gosplan (as one extreme solution) and the magical chaos of market processes (which is placed at the other extreme of the solution continuum). Smart specialisation and its building blocks – centrality of entrepreneurial discovery, strategic interactions between the private sector and the regional agency as well as the evolutionary logic of prioritisation – offer a general solution to coordination problems adapted to a high level of system complexity (such as the EU).

I am among those who think that a certain systemic coherence (at EU level) will emerge from these local processes if the latter are correctly initiated and managed (entrepreneurial discovery) as the diversity of contexts and resources among regions will be reflected by an at least equivalent diversity of projects and new activities, which is exactly what we want.

Smart specialisation strategies and the problem of multilevel coordination

It still has to be accepted that smart specialisation strategy cannot ignore the innovation coordination and orientation attempts (temptations even) at higher political and administrative levels. How can regional smart specialisation strategies be connected with the *meta-priorities* established at national or even European level (see Figure 4.3)? In these times of the 'strategist State' (Aghion and Roulet, 2011), that is a pertinent question. For example, photonics is a *European* priority, like some other key technologies. France has just selected 34 industrial plans. The Netherlands has identified nine priority sectors whose development is envisaged at regional level.[9] Finally, the irruption of societal challenges in political discussions further complicates the general state of the coordination of local, national and European strategies and policies. Beyond the pertinence of all these modalities, also beyond the fact that the processes leading to some of these national or European priorities are far removed from the policy design principles that I established earlier and that allow many inefficiencies to be avoided (Chapter 3), these priorities and grand objectives exist. They can give rise to subsidy and infrastructure programmes that a regional smart specialisation strategy cannot afford to ignore.

Let's return to our Region X. One of the activities selected in this region concerns photonics (see Figure 2.2, Chapter 2), which is also a strategic objective of the EU.[10] For Region X this means the development of applications in the renewable energy field. This activity is indeed a collective exploration of a new domain, led by a group of laboratories and firms. It will – if it

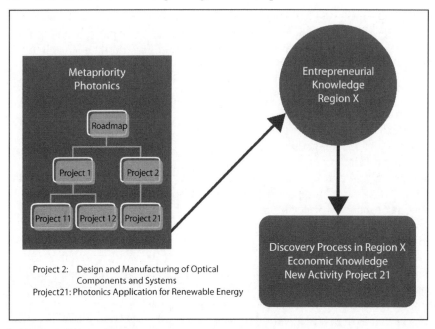

Figure 4.3 Coordination between meta-priorities and regional smart specialisation
strategies

succeeds – allow the competitive positions of these firms to be renewed and
the existing cluster to be freshened up. Above, far above, is the EU's roadmap.

The solution for connecting these different levels is no doubt not to be
sought in the fact that different levels of aggregation are involved. The descrip-
tions given by the roadmap may be subtle and detailed and attain the famous
mid-grained level of granularity that is the pertinent level for the design of
smart specialisation strategies (see Chapter 3). I think the connection is rather
one that links two different spaces – the scientific and technological exploration and experiment space (the roadmap)[11] and the economic exploration and
experiment space (the entrepreneurial discoveries at the heart of the smart
specialisation). Everything that is invented, discovered and experimented
within the science and technology space must be validated economically in
the other space, in which will be discovered what works or doesn't from the
economic point of view. The roadmap is therefore no more and no less than a
well-conceived proposal of technological development options whose economic
pertinence is as yet unknown. Therein lies the role of smart specialisation and
entrepreneurial discoveries.

How is this roadmap used? Either the great architect in Brussels, Belgium,
or Düsseldorf, Germany, (headquarters of the Photonics 21 Secretariat) orga-
nises a sort of immense division of labour – the great European workshop –
to confront all these technological problems systematically, although the

technological solutions thus produced will not necessarily be transformed into economic knowledge. Or the regions concerned (which have recognised skills in these fields) use this roadmap as additional information to situate their capacities and objectives at European level.

Basically, an entrepreneurial discovery process is *informed* by a set of incentive structures and opportunities that exist at all levels of the organisation of economic activity, particularly at local level (for example, the availability of human capital, an appropriate knowledge and skills base), but also of course at national and European levels (markets, competition, certain research or financial resources). Now, the meta-priorities are a part of these opportunities; they generate superior financing possibilities and trigger the creation of service and technology platforms, which can in certain cases generate virtuous spirals of external effects and agglomeration of resources (clusters). This must be taken into consideration in the design processes of a regional smart specialisation strategy. An entrepreneurial discovery project in the photonics field must therefore also be evaluated in relation to the fact that this discovery can be the origin of a new activity that will be part not only of the regional strategy but also the strategic photonic roadmap elaborated at European level.

The basic idea is therefore not necessarily to try to align your smart specialisation strategy with certain meta-priorities. That would be contradictory to the bottom-up and decentralised logic of smart specialisation; entrepreneurial discoveries must have the last word as this is where the economic experiment occurs that will enable the pertinence of a particular technological objective to be validated. It is more a question of taking into account the meta-priorities and the opportunities they offer when the time comes to evaluate and select entrepreneurial discovery projects at regional policy level.

Some meta-priorities – for example, photonics in Europe – are precise and detailed and organised in a well thought-out fashion a set of objectives in the technological reference space. These meta-priorities are important and must be considered by regional decision-makers in charge of the smart specialisation strategy. At regional level, they are informative without being decisive.

4 Summary of Chapter 4

This chapter began with a recapitulation of the objectives of smart specialisation strategy and then deduced some suggestions for developing appropriate ways of measuring the progress achieved. The pertinence of these objectives was discussed according to regional development levels, with particular emphasis on less developed regions. The role and properties of general purpose technologies were examined as an opportunity for less advanced regions to develop new specialities. Finally, the role of smart specialisation strategy as coordination tool in a multilevel system (such as the EU) was touched on, as well as its connection to other types of priorities (grand challenges, national plans, the European roadmap).

Notes

1 Some parts of this chapter draw on Foray and Goenega (2013).
2 Both the OECD (DSTI, TIP steering group) and the RIS3 platform of the IPTS (JRC) are currently deeply involved in the development of an indicator framework. See also the works by K. Debackere (his contribution to the OECD, 2012, report) as well as Wintjes and Hollanders (2011) at UNU-MERIT.
3 On the different logics (or mechanisms) of duplication, see Baruffaldi and Raffo (2014).
4 Of course, more sophisticated taxonomies are useful when the time comes for designing specific programmes to implement the smart specialisation strategy. For example, the *more developed regions* category shows a strong heterogeneity between the top 10 regions and those with a GDP/head close to the average. In other words the rationales and challenges of smart specialisation will be quite different. For more sophisticated taxonomies that could be used to design specific implementation processes see, for example, McCann (2008) who proposes a four-category taxonomy based on three types of criteria (demography, knowledge and urban versus rural). See also the recent exercise by Camagni *et al.* (2014).
5 I borrowed M. Trajtenberg's expression used in his work on development policy (Trajtenberg, 2009).
6 Here, we use the concept of GPTs drawing on the academic literature concerning the economics and econometrics of innovation and growth. While much more technical or analytical, this concept is rather similar to the notion of key enabling technologies (KETs) popularised by the EC.
7 Think of the role of the diaspora as emphasised in Rodrik (2004).
8 Rodrik (2013a) proposes that a growth policy adapted to less advanced countries must focus on two principal areas: the formation of basic capacities (human capital, institutions) and structural change, i.e. the emergence and expansion of new activities potentially rich in innovation and spillovers, and thus the increase in the share of high-productivity sectors.
9 See *The rationale of spatial economic top sector policy*, Statistics Netherlands & PBL Netherlands Environmental Assessment Agency (2012). This report is available at www.pbl.nl/en/publications/the-rationale-of-spatial-economic-top-sector-policy.
10 See *Towards 2020 – Photonics driving economic growth in Europe*, European Technology Platform Photonics 21, Brussels (2013). This report is available at www.photonics21.org/download/Brochures/Photonics_Roadmap_final_lowres.pdf.
11 The Photonics 21 strategic plan comprises six topics, each composed of sub-topics that are more or less translated into research and innovation challenges. The coherence of the overall plan is essentially technological (i.e. this problem has to be resolved before the next one is tackled).

5   Towards practical implementation

The final chapter concerns translating the objectives and principles described in Chapter 3 and Chapter 4 at a certain level of abstraction into practical implementation: a set of tools and programmes that will provide more operational content to the concept. Now there is a change of tone as this chapter builds on the practical experiences that I have accumulated thanks to very close interactions between October 2012 and June 2013 with certain regions that were in the midst of preparations.[1]

First, I will cover the broad outlines of the 'implementation plan' and concrete stages that I described to help the regions to get started. How does one make the tools to support entrepreneurial discovery more operational, to assess smart specialisation potentials and to implement the tools for realising these potentials? I will then address a series of questions frequently asked during the preparation process. Finally, I will tackle the question of the capacities of regional administrations – a question already addressed by Morgan (2013) and that is obviously crucial: a good policy is a policy that can be implemented efficiently and effectively, given the *existing and not imagined* information, incentive and coordination capacities of administrations and regional agencies.

In this respect we must ask how much room for manoeuvre regions have in terms of conceiving the process for establishing priorities, what is flexible and what is non-negotiable. The mode of implementation needs to be flexible with regard to taking into account the specificities of technology, business and framework conditions in a given region but also rigid in its capacity to filter out initiatives and projects that do not have the cumulative and externality properties of smart specialisation and are vulnerable to opportunistic and rent seeking behaviours. Flexibility will require the policy to have a broad view of entrepreneurial discovery, to be pragmatic particularly in regions characterised by poor capabilities and modest innovation performance. Rigidity will require strict methods of *ex ante* evaluation of potentials and *ex-post* measure of progress.

1 How to start?

Chapter 3 and Chapter 4 described programmes at a certain level of abstraction. This means that the definition of a sequence of programmes (maximising entrepreneurial discoveries, inclusive strategy, observation, detection and evaluation, support of early growth, evolving prioritisation), while useful for giving a general sense of what a smart specialisation policy needs to involve, does not really touch on the larger problems of practical implementation. How does one start the process? What are the milestones and the deliverables at each stage?

The difficulty in most cases has been to clarify the difference between the implementation of a smart specialisation strategy and the *modus operandi* of the past. In other words, the regions and their agencies have for about a decade accumulated an intangible form of capital – know-how in terms of the structuring of high-tech sectors (clusters, *pôles de compétitivité*) and a detailed knowledge of the characteristics of these structures. Morgan (2013: p. 107) rightly discusses this form of cognitive path dependence:

> regional governments will not be drafting their smart specialisation strategies in a vacuum, starting from scratch as it were. On the contrary, what regions do in the future partly depends on what they have done in the past, and more importantly on what they have learned from the past.

The difficulty has therefore been to acknowledge this work and make use of it during the exercise, while demonstrating that this structuring work *in itself* could not replace the effort involved in the detection (and construction) of entrepreneurial discovery projects.

First things first: horizontal programmes

As I have already stated, smart specialisation policy and its vertical logic do not replace horizontal policies. The latter are still relevant – particularly those that concern the formation of research and innovation capacities and credit access throughout the regional system. These policies can also concern the development of institutions, which can improve the framework conditions of the economy to the advantage of entrepreneurial dynamism, risk taking and long-term strategies.

Horizontal policies are essential; they contribute to the creation of an *environment* or a climate favourable to entrepreneurial discoveries and thus the smart specialisation dynamic (see Chapter 3).

In relation to horizontal policies, smart specialisation strategy represents a sort of specific and complementary *modus operandi* that will allow something to be accomplished that horizontal policies alone generally do not manage to achieve: a concentration of resources and skills on some new activities that will enable the system to diversify and be transformed.

Defining priorities in a vertical policy: starting with macro-analysis (structures and trends) and vision

Turning to the conception and implementation of the smart specialisation strategy, it is useful to formulate the problem as one of 'smart specialisation diagnostics'[2]: what are the basic obstacles blocking the *desirable structural transformations* in the various contexts of the region and then how do policy-makers come up with *policy solutions*?

To identify desirable structural transformations, it is very helpful to start at the highest level of aggregation to produce a sound analysis of the structures of the economy, its clusters and related trends, entailing some kind of SWOT analysis. Such a preliminary approach needs to involve government and industry as well as other relevant stakeholders. It is useful to conclude such an analysis with the generation of an *allocative rule* that will be determined in accordance with the larger strategic vision that such a macro-analysis will produce – a strategic vision concerning the future of the regional economy. Such a vision concerns not just strength and high-tech clusters. This is a vision regarding an inclusive strategy focusing on both how 'to draw most companies and people into the economic sector of the modern economy' (Phelps, 2012) and how to help the existing modern sector to grow and change. Such a vision will then be translated into the search for (and stimulation of) entrepreneurial discoveries in the domains and areas where structural changes are needed (inclusiveness).

The basic obstacles will include the problem of insufficient resources allocated to entrepreneurial discoveries (informational externalities, uncertainty and capability formation problems), coordination failures and other kinds of market failures (public goods provision, funding gap) that can impede the early growth of the new activities.

This diagnosis (see Figure 5.1) will form the basis of the smart specialisation strategy: for example, we need modernisation of this big (sleeping) sector as well as the diversification of this group of companies and some kind of transition for this segment of a traditional sector. Binding constraints on the desirable structural changes are identified and policy solutions can be derived from the whole exercise.

Let's take a concrete example. In the case of the Basque Country, Spain, there was shown to be a need for structural transformations of the wind energy sector, particularly with regard to the population of firms most threatened by competition from emerging countries (Elola *et al.* 2013). The future of this industry in the Basque Country will therefore depend on the capacity of these firms to undergo modernisation and to diversify towards offshore wind energy, a niche relatively protected from international competition. However, it is a difficult diversification process since it supposes a technological leap. It therefore involves a desirable but difficult structural change owing to a certain number of constraints. A policy of knowledge integration and incentives to entrepreneurial discoveries in this domain should thus be developed to generate new activities that will make this transition possible.

From macro-analysis to selection of priorities at micro-level

The macro-approach, the subsequent strategic vision and the diagnosis alone do not determine the smart specialisation strategy. They determine, so to

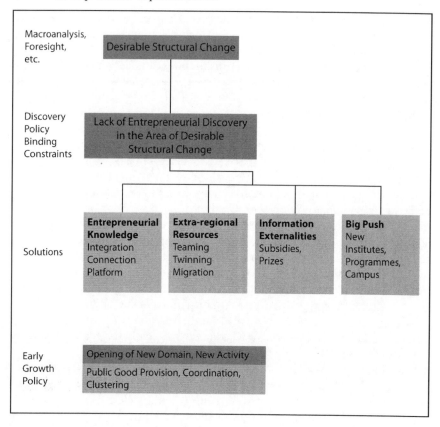

Figure 5.1 A smart specialisation diagnosis

speak, the shape of the smart specialisation budget. On the basis of the allocative rule, it is necessary to observe and detect (and in some cases create the conditions for) the emergence of activities at a mid-grained level of aggregation. Thus the identification of priorities will be based on the macro-analysis and vision (allocative rules) *and* the best knowledge of the local policy-making communities about entrepreneurial discoveries and emerging activities in each of the sectors or between sectors.

By combining the macro-level analysis and the stimulation and observation of micro-dynamics (emerging activities), the strategy will highlight 5–10 priorities, which are likely to be distributed across the whole regional economy according to the allocative rule.

Pace and tempo

As a smart specialisation strategy aims at covering the whole economy to identify good projects, not only from the *excited goblins* (see Chapter 3) but also from other less dynamic actors, the pace and tempo of policy implementation might be different for the different sectors. For example, while policy-makers can start quite early to observe, evaluate and set priorities within the high-tech sector (the *excited goblins* have many good projects!) according to the macro-allocative rule, they need to devote efforts and resources to create the proper conditions for entrepreneurial discoveries in the other sectors. This can be done through a variety of actions (capability formation, calls for pre-investment proposals, building connections with universities, attracting extra-regional resources) before starting to observe, detect, assess and set priorities in these sectors (see Figure 5.2).

After a certain period of time (4–5 years), new priorities emerge and the old ones will no longer be supported through smart specialisation funding. This raises a dilemma as explained in Chapter 3. However, no longer being a priority of the strategy does not mean that this activity, which is now structured, will not receive other kinds of funding. Financing can continue, but logically through the more standard instruments of the horizontal policy (R&D tax credit, innovation costs subsidies, etc.).

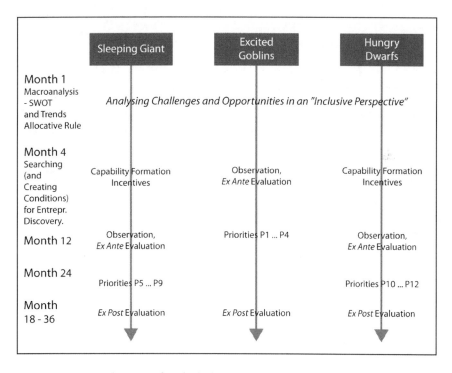

Figure 5.2 Pace and tempo of an inclusive smart specialisation strategy

2 Back from my trips to European regions

During these visits to European regions, I appreciated the capacity of each region to invent its own approach to identifying its future priority domains, each one endeavouring to follow the spirit and the letter of the exercise (first the structural analysis, SWOT, etc., then the detection of entrepreneurial discovery projects). Of course, the first part of the exercise is easier than the second.

What regions do well ... and less well

Almost all regions are good at making a diagnosis that results in a thematic or topical structure (clusters, *pôles de compétitivité*, synergies and intersections, etc.). However, it is difficult to make it clear that this is just a starting point of the process. A step further means that after this structural exercise there remains the task of identifying (or constructing) the entrepreneurial discovery projects. Presenting only a thematic structure as a smart specialisation plan is a failure because firms' implications, projects and the potential move towards real structural effects remain invisible or unknown. A structure is a structure. This is static. By definition, a smart specialisation strategy is not a structure but a process, and as a process it will generate a new (more diversified) structure.

The gold digger's map is no use if he doesn't want to dig!

Beyond the diversity of approaches, I have observed, *grosso modo*, two operational methods:

1   Regional administrations that call upon the business and research world early on in the process to collect information about future projects, with this information representing the basis for the elaboration of strategic or thematic domains.
2   Regions that begin with a 'home-grown' theme-construction exercise based on systematic evidence (publications, patents, etc.) before calling on the world of business and research concerned by each of the identified themes.

I think both these approaches are valid in practice. They each have advantages and disadvantages. The first has the merit of faithfully respecting the (bottom-up) philosophy of smart specialisation strategy but the disadvantage of creating enormous informational complexity. It involves a considerable task of subsequent analysis and simplification that entails certain risks.

The second approach has the great merit of fairly quickly reducing complexity (an important point in large, economically advanced regions: Ile de France, France; London, United Kingdom; Baden Würtemberg, Germany; Catalonia, Spain) but it poses the risk of overlooking certain themes that cannot be detected within the standard framework of indicators (publications, patents), a problem for a strategy that should be inclusive.

In each instance, the result is a mapping of strategic domains. All the regions have done it but the map – although useful – cannot be considered a substitute for strategy. The level of description of the domains is usually too coarse-grained. Certain domains – while interesting on paper – in reality contain no entrepreneurial dynamic or the impact of potential transformations by research and innovation would be too weak for the regional economy.

We must therefore take this map for what it is: an exploratory tool, certainly useful for the gold diggers that we are, but ultimately insufficient. The map shows us where we have to dig. Without the map we would dig almost anywhere and it would be pretty ineffective. Thanks to the map, we know more or less where we might find mineral deposits, in other words – in our case – entrepreneurial discovery projects.

To take a fictitious example, the map will identify the domain *energy efficiency of buildings and integration of the wood sector*. The granularity is pertinent and shows us clearly where to dig. Indeed, we have to carry on digging to detect projects, identify partners, and formulate four- or five-year application objectives. We dig to define the collective entrepreneurial discovery project.

The map is thus a precious tool for the gold digger, but having the map does not mean the end of prospecting. He cannot stop there. Let's also note that the map is not the territory. Are all the important domains to be explored really there, indicated on the map? Or might some of them have eluded analysis since they remain largely undetectable by standard indicators?

Thus, in most regions, there is a critical moment of moving from the 'easy-to-do' structural analysis and science and technology mapping to the 'hard-to-do' entrepreneurial discovery/new activity identification. Limiting the elaboration of a smart specialisation strategy to a simple identification of scientific and technological structures and topics is comfortable: you can include everything in the topics and this will make the life of the politicians easier. Themes have a certain elasticity. For example, let's take a single firm that is innovative in a narrow niche of renewable energy based on biomass production; the region cannot adopt it as a new speciality because there is only one actor but the firm is a local champion and we would like to put it in the showcase. So let's create a broad theme (biology and energy) and we can put it in. However, we cannot call this smart specialisation. This is just a (more sophisticated) way of spreading the money.

The passage from structural analysis of clusters, strengths, synergies, etc. to the identification of entrepreneurial discovery projects is the main issue: it is both crucial and difficult. The mental vision of a regional politician is to put 'all the good things' in the smart specialisation showcase (for good and bad reasons). However, the real point is not to select all the good things but the best projects; those which promise the highest payoffs in terms of structural changes.

How to fail

You will fail at the exercise if you write the strategy first. Writing it first means that the a priori vision and knowledge you have of the system (often extensive knowledge thanks to the preceding efforts of structuring and measuring the profiles of scientific and technological specialisation) seem to suffice when writing the future strategy. Writing it first can be done in different ways:

- You just present grand themes, which of course really do reflect the strong points and offer the immense advantage of being able to integrate a large number of actors and organisations, thus settling quite a few political problems. However, these themes do not reflect the entrepreneurial discovery dimension, the real degree of involvement of companies or the relative proximity to the market. 'Here's my strategy: biotechnology and environment; health, information technology and dependency; advanced materials and optics'. But that won't work. What's being described here is the starting point, not the result of the exercise.
- You just present the strong points of public research. Yet the strategy cannot be reduced to a mechanism for strengthening existing public research capacities (even though it was an important way of spending the structural funds allocated to regional development in recent years). Smart specialisation strategy is, on a far broader scale, a tool of economic development by research and innovation that must associate all the actors in projects whose centre of gravity is represented by companies.
- You simply recycle cluster programmes. We can of course hope that from these clusters will emerge projects driven by entrepreneurial discovery associating research and companies to explore avenues of potential development and transformation. However, nothing is inevitable or automatic. All will depend on the vigour and quality of the entrepreneurial discovery projects, within these clusters but also elsewhere (outside the high-tech clusters).

So, we can see that a fundamental cause of failure lies in presenting what already exists – structures, strong points – without taking into account the importance of entrepreneurial discovery. To avoid failure, you must therefore go a step beyond the structuring processes already undertaken in order to identify what within these structures (or elsewhere) can get the system *moving*, transform and diversify it.

Some interesting – and common – cases

I would like to finish this chapter by addressing some questions frequently asked by stakeholders (from the regional administration, universities or firms) and which this book has not yet completely answered.

Châteaux and cathedrals, mountains and beaches: tourism in
smart specialisation strategy

I would like to talk again about the case of tourism as a possible priority as it is one that interests many regions and, furthermore, we have turned it into a sort of *textbook case* to illustrate that in numerous regions, certain activities linked with tourism can be promoted to the rank of strategic priority. This would bring about the development of a certain research, technology and innovation activity (no doubt based on ICTs) to improve the efficiency of the tourist service, or the development of certain digital skills to transform its range of services, or the elaboration of certain technological knowledge for the purpose of heritage preservation. All this would make a good impression in the regional showcase that wishes to display the strengths and assets of the region. Indeed, such a priority allows us to pursue the two objectives that we have always associated: improve the performances of a sector (tourism in this case) by research, innovation and structural change; and (incidentally) build new invention and innovation capacities to conquer a certain market niche (here the development of ICT application for a particular tourist service). A case in point is the Centre Region – a region of France that has important tourism activities thanks to the chateaux of the Loire Valley. Château de Chambord and Château de Chenonceau will no doubt look good in the smart specialisation showcase. However, when we look closer, as the Centre Region did, we notice that nearly all the companies that might be concerned by this process of entre-preneurial discovery and new activity development are outside the region – not far away (Île de France), but not there. Nonetheless, should priority still be given to Chambord, Chenonceau and the others? A difficult question.

Indeed, activities and companies outside the region are going to be mas-sively financed in order to improve tourist facilities. I am not suggesting these facilities should not be improved; this must no doubt be done within the fra-mework of a sectoral policy but not within the framework of regional smart specialisation strategy. Of course, it has been said many times that the estab-lishment of a priority does not make it essential that all the necessary resources for the new activity should be available within the region; of course not, and all combinations between intra-regional and extra-regional resources are possible. However, the presence of a minimum number of strengths and dynamic actors in the region is essential, otherwise we would be building on sand. Naturally, tourist facilities will be improved but no new capacity will have been generated for the region. In short, let's not confuse the beautiful *objects* we have and that we would like to display (châteaux and cathedrals, beaches and mountains, vineyards) but that have no part to play in the smart specialisation strategy with the beautiful *projects* that, through research and innovation, aim to transform the activities associated with showing these objects off to their best advantage. When these projects exist, and if their centre of gravity is actually in the region in question, then they have every reason to be in the regional strategy showcase.

The role of public research organisations and universities

In many regions I met those responsible for universities and public research centres, who feel almost threatened by the new approach. Indeed, they believe that it jeopardises a source of financing of universities and research infrastructures (namely, the European Regional Development Fund – ERDF) that they were accustomed to using copiously.

Naturally, universities and public research organisations (PROs) will continue to play a large role. However, it is less central. The centre of gravity of the smart specialisation dynamic is the firms since they are best placed to conduct entrepreneurial discovery processes. In fact, the principle of smart specialisation strategy cannot be reduced to a tool for strengthening existing public research capacities to finance laboratories and equipment, which is what university lobbies in the regions tend to think. The strategy is much more broadly a tool for economic development through research and innovation that must associate all the actors concerned in projects not necessarily centred on public research or universities.

Here, we are reminded of the works of Paula Stephan (Sumell *et al.*, 2009) concerning the famous Midwest Syndrome:[3] the states of the Midwest of the USA invest a great deal in their universities and doctoral training but then retain very few students seeking their first job. Most of them travel to the East or West coasts. Overall, only one-quarter of students trained in the Midwest actually stay there. In certain states (Indiana, Iowa), the brain drain is severe. Certain areas with a strong tradition of training students for industry (such as Urbana-Champaign, Illinois, Lafayette, Pennsylvania) subsequently manage to employ only 3% of these freshly qualified PhDs. Thus, we see that excellent universities and generous financing for higher-education programmes do not suffice to create the corresponding employment. Another essential factor is the capacity of firms to collectively develop new specialities and generate structural change via research and innovation.

However, even if the role of universities is not central, it is nonetheless large. As demonstrated clearly by Goddard *et al.* (2013) in an article devoted to this subject, universities and PROs will be the essential actors in knowledge integration processes (see Figure 2.1, Chapter 2), especially in regions where firms have poor research and innovation capacities. Local universities and regional PRO agencies will therefore have a particular responsibility in terms of interactions and collaborations with industrial and service firms to encourage the emergence of new exploration and experimentation activities and initiate structural change. The example of the French National Institute for Agricultural Research (INRA) is revealing. INRA has regional agencies in many places. Who can contribute better to stimulating the agrofood sector through research and innovation? Who, faced with this deeply *sleeping giant*, can have a strategic vision regarding what should be done to make the transition to the agriculture of the future and thus be the architect and initiator of entrepreneurial discovery projects that would speed up the desired transformations (see Box 5.1)?

Box 5.1 The example of the role of the French National Institute for Agricultural Research

A meeting in Paris (19 December 2012) with the regional directors of INRA gave me the opportunity to reflect on the role of public research bodies in smart specialisation strategies. Knowing that INRA is extremely active in the regions and presents itself as an active partner of firms in the agriculture, agrofood and other sectors, one may wonder what skills this body can contribute to the elaboration of regional strategies. Each region is expected to elaborate a strategic vision of its future, an inclusive strategy through which it identifies certain objectives regarding structural transformations: awaken the *sleeping giant* or further mobilise the *excited goblins* thanks to the prioritisation of certain innovative projects. 'I'd like to stimulate all that a bit', thinks the Regional Council, 'but how and why?' This is where INRA must provide its skills concerning the future of the agrofood industry, and the essential technological and organisational transitions that will only be achieved through innovation.

By combining the strategic vision of the future of the region (that the region must create) and the strategic vision of the future of the agrofood and agriculture sectors (that INRA can provide), we will be able to identify the domains in which new activities should emerge without delay. There are, for example, basic professional transformations that must be initiated, which INRA can anticipate and which certain regions must include in their strategy, because these sectors count for these regions. In domains perhaps less structured than others in terms of clusters and entrepreneurial capacities, INRA must provide the expertise that will show where stimulus is needed and where good projects can be found.

Afterwards, as we emphasised in the previous section, this macro-analysis of structures and trends that identifies potential domains for prioritisation must be validated by the quality of entrepreneurial discoveries and projects. However, here again the PRO can and must play a stimulating role: partnership, networking and any other mechanism aimed at activating these discovery and exploration processes.

The system of large, national-level research bodies is certainly an asset for the regions, providing that these bodies learn to create the right balance between strategic missions of *national* interest and those that consist of serving the emergence of *local* innovation systems (smart specialisation strategy); two missions that are not necessarily compatible, as we well know. Finding the right balance to reconcile a national strategy with the capacity to respond to local opportunities no doubt requires a renewal of the ways in which these large bodies are organised.

Thus, local universities and regional PRO agencies have an important role to play and can benefit from financing for smart specialisation strategy but only within the framework of their contribution to and association with the entrepreneurial discovery processes. Local universities should be quite naturally in step with smart specialisation strategy within the context of their third mission: knowledge transfer, collaboration with the world of industry and services, economic development aid, etc. (Héraud and Levy, 2005; Foray and Lissoni, 2010). In the long term, of course, all missions are pertinent as the smart specialisation dynamic thrives on new knowledge (first mission) and a sufficient supply of qualified persons in the new domains (second mission). However, within the next 5–7 years, what is *essential* for the smart specialisation strategy is not so much basic research, the outcome of which will not be apparent for many years, as strongly application-oriented programmes and laboratories that as such constitute key partners in entrepreneurial discovery processes; those that must happen *now*.

A dispersed strategy?

Another issue has often arisen: a strategy that embraces the best entrepreneurial discovery projects, conceived here and there throughout the system, is inevitably dispersed and not coherent, compared to a strategy focused on high-tech innovations, for example. We can of course think that, but it is the price we pay for a strategy whose prime objective is diversification of the economy and the generation of new options. The coherence of this strategy is less apparent but nonetheless very real. Ideally, we will find in the strategy a set of *new discovery and exploration activities*, linked to existing productive structures in order to transform them through research and innovation.

National or regional strategies?

In many cases, I have observed very poor administrative and governance capacities at the regional level. In such instances, the strategy needs to be designed and implemented at national level. This is perfectly fine in such circumstances and a national strategy is likely to deliver similar outcomes (in terms of entrepreneurial discoveries, new activities and structural changes) to a regional strategy. However, it is certainly less easy for policy makers in the national government to resist the temptation to use the strategy as a tool for the elaboration of a top-down plan that will dictate to each region what its role and place are to be in the *grand plan national*! If the national government does not resist the temptation, or more simply misunderstands and misuses the concept, the national strategy will be a failure. A national strategy is therefore only acceptable because of institutional deficits at regional level and if there is a strong political commitment on the part of the national agency to respect and preserve the essence of the smart specialisation strategy: the discovery process is an integral part of the political action and must be carried out within the framework of strategic interaction between the government and private sector.

How could we define good regional government in view of the tasks and responsibilities created by a smart specialisation strategy?

The first idea is innovation. Designing and implementing a smart specialisation strategy represents a range of process and product innovations that the regional agency must generate and manage. The *innovation culture* is essential, since a smart specialisation strategy causes certain abrupt changes in policy know-how and practices. These abrupt changes, which may result in organisational crises, can only be managed by innovation. We know how hard it is to innovate, the obstacles and disincentives that characterise the public sector in this respect (Borins, 2008). In order to implement a large-scale innovation programme – such as that represented by smart specialisation strategy – we must therefore both acknowledge the limits of the policy instruments used until now, favour an approach whereby innovation in practices and instruments is generated as the strategy develops, and display creativity and flexibility. The role of 'local heroes' – the senior managers in public administration who believe in the new strategy and create the internal conditions favourable to its implementation – is vital (Kelman, 2008).

The second idea, well defended by Rodrik (2013b) and Sabel (2004), has already been mentioned: it involves guarding against the dangerous illusion of believing that we already know what should be done and that the strategy can be limited to setting up incentives to ensure that 'what should be done and what we already know' is achieved. This logic of the principal agent knowing practically everything is not appropriate and does not work. Good regional government must thus place at the heart of its strategy the interactions between the administration and the private sector that will enable us to discover what must be done. Rodrik (2013b) uses the notion of 'embeddedness' to describe a high intensity of communication and interaction and also a form of informational intelligence that will enable the government to gradually acquire information and knowledge regarding the new activities and new domains opened and explored by the private sector. It is also this form of interlinking that will slowly win support for the strategy from all the social groups concerned.

The third idea concerns an *experimentalist culture*, a culture of risk and evaluation. By definition, a smart specialisation strategy should not finance projects certain of success even if it is a temptation for the politician (Stiglitz and Wallsten, 1999). The objective is to help risky and difficult projects to develop. Risky projects, not because they deal with fundamental research, but because the new domain of innovations and structural transformations is not known and the economic knowledge relating to it has not yet been produced. Risky projects too since their results are only imperfectly appropriable by those who initiated them. It is therefore a question of detecting entrepreneurial discovery projects characterised by a *negative correlation* between (high) social and (low) private returns (Trajtenberg, 2012). Onto this risk culture must be grafted an evaluation culture. The regional agency must endeavour to develop this culture and put in place the indicators and methods to evaluate potentials and measure progress.

Finally, the last idea concerns the regional agency's capacity to have a *dynamic and long-term vision*. The problem is not to choose once and for all priorities that would hamper the system on a long-term basis and that would be sufficiently broad to satisfy everyone. The problem is to set up a process that will facilitate the revision of the priorities themselves and the reallocation of resources between activities as time passes. What is important is not what is chosen at the time (mistakes can and will be made) but the operational mode that will allow the constant generation (and facilitate the development) of new options. However, isn't this too much to ask of regional agencies, which in many countries remain relatively weak and underdeveloped?

3 The challenge of regional administrative capabilities

In his important article concerning the theory of new industrial policies, Rodrik (2004) is quite optimistic regarding the capacities of public administrations to implement a sophisticated policy concept: 'It is common to complain about incompetence and corruption in government bureaucracies. But bureaucratic competence varies greatly among different agencies within the same country, and most countries have some pockets of bureaucratic competence.'

Indeed, the concrete process we have described above will be particularly demanding in terms of policy-making capability, and smart specialisation strategies will not succeed in Europe if policy-making capability at regional level does not reach a high level of competence and commitment. This is no surprise: smart specialisation is part of the so-called *new industrial policy* family that aims at designing and deploying sophisticated instruments to make compatible vertical choices for concentrating resources and market dynamics. The policy challenge is enormous. Unlike Rodrick, Morgan (2013: p. 106) makes it a possible factor of failure:

> the ideal governance structure would include new stakeholders from the worlds of business and civil society, selected for their competence in the network rather than their status in the hierarchy, and this is a radical innovation in its own right because it runs counter to everything we know about how regional elites usually deploy their power and patronage, especially in the face of novelty.

I will position myself halfway between the opposing opinions expressed by these two authors, while acknowledging both the difficulty of this problem and the opportunities it offers with regard to new capacity formation in administrations. There is an endogenous skill development process triggered by the interest and finesse of the concept itself. I have observed it in tangible form in the regions.

Indeed, we need to see this challenge as an opportunity for improving human capital and creating pockets of bureaucratic excellence in regional administrations. We have already observed how smart specialisation goals can generate great motivation and commitment on the part of regional policy-makers since smart specialisation strategy opens up new policy opportunities that can have a real impact on the future of regions through the deployment of sophisticated programmes. There are multiple examples of methodological innovations, for example, in relation to the observation mechanisms set up to detect entrepreneurial discovery projects. It seems to me that these innovations and this motivation have a dual source: on the one hand, the fact that the concept of smart specialisation policy offers regional administrations the possibility of shaping the innovation system without perverting or weakening the economic dynamics; on the other hand, a new generation of civil servants – well trained, composed of people who have at some time completed a Masters or doctoral thesis in economics and innovation management – assumes responsibility for executing the plan with enthusiasm. This is a generation that gives the impression that this is all that it was waiting for: a difficult but exciting policy project in the domain of innovation and competitiveness.[4]

4 The value of smart specialisation policy in the GVC age

Baldwin (2011) adopts an extreme position with regard to the changing nature of globalisation – which has been triggered by the so-called '2nd unbundling phenomenon': largely because of the development of new digital technologies, global value chains (GVCs) have become the dominant mode of governance in manufacturing and service sectors as well as the main locus of innovation in which learning and upgrading processes occur fairly easily and rapidly. Thus, joining a GVC 'could create advanced manufacturing activity in a developing nation in a matter of months.' (Baldwin, 2011, p. 6). Although anecdotal evidence as well as case studies show that the scope and extent of learning and upgrading within GVCs are conditional on many factors and that a rapid and complete learning process is certainly not taken for granted just because it happens within a GVC (see Humphrey and Schmitz, 2002; Schmitz and Knorringa, 2000), Baldwin's provocative ideas indicate a certain way of thinking about industrial policy. Industrial policy is no longer rejected because of the well-known failures of the practice of sectoral prioritisation; it is now discarded because there is no longer any point in trying to create local industries or activities through a place-based policy approach. Baldwin therefore considered policy prescriptions derived from the local systems of innovation/ smart specialisation literature and the GVC literature as being diametrically opposed! It is perhaps useful to acknowledge that the conceptual compatibility is much more obvious between a smart specialisation approach and the concept of global innovation networks – as our section on the space and networks of smart specialisation has demonstrated.

The point here is not to discuss the accuracy of Baldwin's representation of the process of innovation in a global economy, but rather to challenge the very idea that "joining GVCs" as a mode of learning and capacity building is becoming the only successful growth strategy and that any other type of policy approach should therefore be discarded. In contrast to Baldwin's statement, the smart specialisation literature is based on the idea that there is a strong economic case for building and developing local systems of innovation because the colocation of research, firms and labour forces, if adequately stimulated, is a fundamental engine for entrepreneurial discovery and structural changes.

And finally, isn't the fundamental question underlying this discussion one of economic power in the area of innovation and competitiveness? Do we want to shift this power from global multinational buyers to local (but open) networks of actors and, if so, how?

5 Summary of Chapter 5

This chapter essentially addressed the initial feedback acquired from certain regions engaged in the preparation of their smart specialisation strategy. It presented a simple execution plan for the strategy, used in numerous regions, and discussed a certain number of difficulties that have arisen during the practical implementation phase of the concept. The chapter ended with the problem of the capacities and skills of regional administrations in charge of strategy implementation.

Notes

1 The regions in France with which I have worked closely are: Alsace, Aquitaine, Centre, Île de France, Limousin and Rhône-Alpes. I have also had interactions with Languedoc-Roussillon, Midi-Pyrénées, Provence-Alpes-Côte d'Azur and Nord-Pas-de-Calais. They are all French-speaking regions as at a certain level of in-depth work and dialogue, use of the mother tongue becomes essential and English no longer suffices. However, I have also had the chance to observe many other European regions, particularly within the context of peer reviews organised by the S3 Platform in Seville, Spain.
2 See the works by R. Hausmann, D. Rodrik and others on growth strategies and growth diagnostics. For example. Hausmann *et al.* (2008).
3 It should be noted that the data used in this work concerning the 'industrial' placement of PhDs are not recent but from 1997–99.
4 We must also salute the mechanism of peer reviews set up by the S3 Platform at the Institute for Prospective Technological Studies (IPTS) in Seville, Spain – a rather effective mechanism that strengthens the mobilisation, motivation and skills of participants.

Conclusion

The fact that I asked M. Trajtenberg to write the Foreword for this book is significant, beyond my admiration for him and our friendship. It demonstrates that the concept of smart specialisation strategy is primarily a generic tool for innovation policy and structural change; in other words, it is not restricted to any particular level of geographic and/or administrative organisation. If the concept is well understood and implemented – it involves implementing actions to assist the development of new specialities that will trigger structural change via research and innovation and these actions focus on the promotion and detection of entrepreneurial discovery projects and the local concentration of resources relating to these projects – it can be applied without any problem to a particular sector as well as any geographic or political entity.

Having said that, the regional level seems particularly pertinent since the exacting requirements for information and coordination imposed by the design of this strategy seem more easily fulfilled at this level, providing that regional agencies have the necessary capacities and skills available. This is why the encounter between the smart specialisation strategy approach and regional policies *struck the right note* in innovation policy circles, especially in Brussels, Belgium, but also at the Organisation for Economic Co-operation and Development (OECD) or the World Bank, just as, it seems to me, D. Rodrik's new industrial policy *struck the right note* in development economics and policy.

Obviously the *right note* was loud and clear and the European Commission's (EC) promptness in applying this approach in all European regions as *ex-ante conditionality* has given it great impact and visibility. This promptness can be criticised, as the doubtlessly necessary testing and pilot study stages have not been carried out. On the other hand, it can also be said that regional actors were waiting for this new challenge after years of rather routine management of structural funds devoted to R&D and innovation. Suddenly, the concept of smart specialisation strategy engenders creativity, imagination and the formulation of a collective vision that must be translated into regional strategy, which must in turn respect certain conditions in order to avoid distortions and stimulate decentralised discovery, experimentation and innovation processes.

The smart specialisation strategy concept is demanding but also offers many benefits and my tour of European regions convinced me that this concept appeared at the right time to satisfy the intellectual ambitions and strategic challenges of a large number of innovation actors all over Europe. In many regions, the launching of the strategy has aroused intense mobilisation and a certain fervour: having to think collectively about the region's future in the knowledge economy, to do so at the pertinent level of granularity, and finally to do so in an inclusive way, allows each region to uncover hitherto hidden intangible treasures and to outline promising new avenues for development. In many regions, the aims of the strategy and its operational content have been clearly understood and the main actors have thus adhered to it with enthusiasm.[1]

One evening in November 2013, upon my return from Brussels, where the concept was presented and discussed during a major conference at the European Parliament introduced by the President of the European Council and two Commissioners,[2] I was considering the brilliant career of a relatively simple idea, almost immediate implementation of which has enabled numerous refinements and detailed specifications to be made; quite a rare destiny, no doubt owing less to the *ex ante* sophistication of the idea than the fact that it was produced at the right moment and that it will encounter different groups of extremely motivated actors. The characteristics of this success therefore elicit modesty. I am aware that numerous ideas regarding technological policy and innovation, far more sophisticated or shrewd than this one, have been less fortunate and never achieved a breakthrough, have been lost somewhere in the vast space of translating concept into practice, have disappeared forever for reasons that I have attempted to formulate elsewhere (Foray, 2012).

That is why the EC's promptness in implementing the smart specialisation strategy concept can be understood and appreciated in this light, as it has enabled this concept to avoid the fate of being buried in the great cemetery of good ideas that were never tested or applied. The gigantic laboratory of the European regions is now operating at full capacity. We shall soon know whether the development and application of this concept in the conditions prevailing from 2010–14 have proved beneficial to regional innovation systems.

Notes

1 Mention must be made here of the first systematic study concerning the implantation process of the strategy conducted in 2013 by the ISI (Karlsruhe) among 500 persons responsible for regional policy throughout Europe (Kroll, 2013). In particular, this study establishes that the RIS3 policy approach has been remarkably positively received and stresses the importance of safeguarding the surprisingly strong initial openness of the regions. This conclusion must of course be qualified to some extent (especially concerning the lack of private co-financing) but the overall impression regarding the way in which regions have grasped the concept and achieved its implantation is very positive.

2 High-Level Conference under the patronage of Herman Achille Van Rompuy, President of the European Council: *Regions as motors of new growth through smart specialisation*, European Parliament, Brussels, 8 November 2013. This was also the occasion of the launching of the *Vanguard Initiative: New Growth by Smart Specialisation* by the Government of Flanders, Belgium.

References

P. Aghion, 'A Primer on Innovation and Growth', *Bruegel Policy Brief*, 6, 2006.

P. Aghion, 'Innovation Process and Policy: What Do We Learn from New Growth Theory?' in J. Lerner and S. Stern (eds), *The Rate and Direction of Inventive Activity Revisited.*, Chicago, IL: NBER, University of Chicago Press, 2012.

P. Aghion, J. Boulanger and E. Cohen, 'Rethinking Industrial Policy', *Bruegel Policy Brief*, 4, 2011.

P. Aghion, P.A. David and D. Foray, 'Science, Technology and Innovation for Economic Growth: Linking Policy Research and Practice', *Research Policy*, 38(4), 2009, pp. 681–693.

P. Aghion and A. Roulet, *Repenser l'Etat: Pour une nouvelle social démocratie.* Paris: Seuil, 2011.

A. Agrawal and I. Cockburn, 'University Research, Industrial R&D and the Anchor Tenant Hypothesis', *International Journal of Industrial Organization*, 21(9), 2003, pp. 1417–1433.

A. Agrawal, I. Cockburn and A. Oettl, 'Why are Some Regions More Innovative than Others? The Role of Firm Size Diversity,' NBER Working Paper, 17793, 2010.

A. Agrawal, I. Cockburn and C. Rosell, 'Not Invented Here? Innovation in Company Towns', *Journal of Urban Economics*, 67(1), 2010, pp. 78–89.

D. Ahner and M. Landabaso, 'Regional Policies in Times of Austerity', *European Review of Industrial Economics and Policy*, 2, 2011.

G. Aichholzer, 'Delphi Austria: an Example of Tailoring Foresight to the Needs of a Small Country'. Paper presented at the Regional Conference on Technology Foresight, UNIDO, Vienna, 2001.

A. Amin and P. Cohendet, *Architectures of Knowledge: Firms, Capabilities and Knowledge.* Oxford: Oxford University Press, 2004.

C. Antonelli, *The Economics of Innovation, New Technologies and Structural Change.* London: Routledge, 2002.

K. Arrow, 'Economic Welfare and the Allocation of Resources for Invention', in R. Nelson (ed.), *The Rate and Direction of Inventive Activity: Economic and Social Factors.* Cambridge, MA: National Bureau Committee for Economic Research, 1962.

D. Audretsch and M. Feldman, 'R&D Spillovers and the Geography of Innovation and Production', *American Economic Review*, 86(3), 1996, pp. 630–640.

D. Bailey and S. MacNeil, 'The Rover Task Force: A case study in proactive and reactive policy intervention?', *Regional Science Policy & Practice* 1(1), 2009, pp. 109–124.

R. Baldwin, 'Trade And Industrialisation After Globalisation's 2nd Unbundling: How Building And Joining A Supply Chain Are Different And Why It Matters, *NBER working paper series*, 17716, 2011.

F. Barca, *An Agenda for a Reformed Cohesion Policy: a place-based approach to meeting European Union challenges and expectations*. Independent Report prepared at the request of the Commissioner for Regional Policy. D. Hübner. Brussels: European Commission, 2009.

S. Baruffaldi and J. Raffo, *The Geography of Duplicated Inventions: an Analysis from Patent Citations*, draft, Lausanne: Ecole Polytechnique Fédérale de Lausanne, 2014.

F. Barca, P. McCann and P. Rodriguez-Pose, 'The Case for Regional Development Intervention: Place-based versus place-neutral approaches', *Journal of Regional Science*, 52(1), 2012, pp. 134–152.

Basque Government, 'Estrategias de especializacion inteligente', *Ekonomiaz 83*, II, 2013.

W. Baumol, *The Free-market Innovation Machine: Analyzing the Growth Miracle of Capitalism*. Princeton, NJ: Princeton University Press, 2002.

S. Berger, *Making in America: From Innovation to Market*. Cambridge, MA: MIT Press, 2013.

S. Borins (ed.), *Innovations in Government: Research, Recognition and Replication*. Washington, DC: Brookings Institution Press, 2008.

R. Boschma and K. Frenken, 'Technological Relatedness and Regional Branching', in H. Bathelt, M. Feldman and D. Kogler (eds), *Beyond Territory: Dynamic Geographies of Knowledge Creation, Diffusion and Innovation*. Abingdon: Routledge, 2011.

S. Breschi and F. Lissoni, '"Cross-firm" Inventors and Social Networks: Localized Knowledge Spillovers Revisited', *Annales d'Economie et de Statistique*, 79/80, 2005, pp. 189–209.

T. Bresnahan, 'The Mechanisms of Information Technology's Contribution to Economic Growth', in J.-P. Touffut (ed.), *Institutions, Innovation and Growth*. Cheltenham: Edward Elgar, 2003.

T. Bresnahan, 'General Purpose Technologies', in B. Hall and N. Rosenberg (eds), *Handbook in Economics of Innovation*, 2. Amsterdam: North-Holland, 2010.

T. Bresnahan, 'Generality, Recombination and Reuse', in J. Lerner and S. Stern (eds), *The Rate and Direction of Inventive Activity Revisited*. Chicago, IL: NBER, University of Chicago Press, 2012.

T. Bresnahan, A. Gambardella and A. Saxenian, '"Old Economy" Inputs for "New Economy" Outcomes: Cluster Formation in the New Silicon Valleys', *Industrial and Corporate Change*, 10(4), 2001, pp. 835–860.

T. Bresnahan and M. Trajtenberg, 'General Purpose Technologies: Engines of Growth', *Journal of Econometrics*, 65(1), 1995, pp. 83–108.

R. Camagni, R. Capello and C. Lenzi, 'A Territorial Taxonomy of Innovative Regions and the European Regional Policy Reforms: Smart Innovation Policies', *Scienze Regionali*, 13(1), 2014.

R. Capello (ed.), 'Smart Specialisation and the new EU Cohesion Policy Reform', *Scienze Regionali*, 13(1), 2014.

A. Chatterji, E. Glaeser and W. Kerr, 'Clusters of Entrepreneurship and Innovation', NBER Working Paper, 13-090, 2013.

P. Dasgupta, 'The Welfare Economics of Knowledge Production', *Oxford Review of Economic Policy*, 4(4), 1988, pp. 1–12.

P.A. David, 'The Economics of Locational Tournaments', *Sillicon Valley Research Project*, Discussion Paper 1. Stanford, CA: CEPR, Stanford University, 1984.

P.A. David, 'Krugman's Geography of Development: NEGs, POGs and Naked Models in Space', *International Regional Science Review*, 22, 1999, pp. 162–172.

P.A. David, 'Path-Dependence in Economic Processes: Implications for policy analysis in dynamical system contexts', in K. Dopfer (ed.), *The Evolutionary Foundations of Economics*. Cambridge: Cambridge University Press, 2005.

P.A. David, 'Comments' in *Enhancing Bulgaria's competitiveness and export performance through technology absorption and innovation*, World Bank Report, 2010.

P.A. David and S. Metcalfe, 'How the Universities Can Best Contribute to Enhancing Europe's Innovative Performance?' in *Knowledge for Growth: Prospects for Science, Technology and Innovation*, Report, EUR 24047, European Union, 2009.

P.A. David and G. Wright, 'General Purpose Technologies and Surges in Productivity: Historical Reflections on the Future of the ICT Revolution'. *Oxford Economic and Social History Working Paper*, 1999-W31, Oxford, 1999.

G. Duranton, 'California Dreamin': the Feeble Case for Cluster Policies', *Review of Economic Analysis*, 3(1), 2011, pp. 3–45.

A. Elola, M.D. Parrilli and R. Rabellotti, 'The Resilience of Clusters in the Context of Increasing Globalization: the Basque Wind Energy Value Chain', *European Planning Studies*, 21(7), 2013, pp. 1–18.

European Commission, *Regional Innovation Strategies under the European Regional Development Fund Innovative Actions 2000–2002*. Luxembourg: Office for Official Publications of the European Communities, 2002.

European Commission, *Guide to Research and Innovation Strategy for Smart Specialisation*. D. Foray, J. Goddard, X. Goenaga, M. Landabaso, P. McCann, K. Morgan, F. Mulatero, C. Nauwelaers, R. Ortega-Argilés. Seville: Joint Research Centre-IPTS, 2012a.

European Commission, *Revision of the state aid rules for research and development and innovation*, Issues paper. Brussels: Competition Directorate-Geneneral for Competition, 2012b

M. Feldman and J. Francis, 'Entrepreneurs and the formation of industrial clusters'. Paper presented at the Conference on Complexity and Industrial Clusters, Fondazione Montedison, Milan, June 2001.

L. Fleming, C. King and A. Juda, 'Small Worlds and Regional Innovation', *Organization Science*, 18, 2007, pp. 938–954.

D. Foray, *The Economics of Knowledge*. Cambridge, MA: MIT Press, 2004.

D. Foray, 'Structuring a Policy Response to a 'Grand Challenge', in *Knowledge for Growth: Prospects for Science, Technology and Innovation*, Report, EUR 24047, European Union, 2009.

D. Foray, 'Why is it so Difficult to Translate Innovation Economics into Useful and Applicable Policy Prescriptions?', in J. Lerner and S. Stern (eds), *The Rate and Direction of Inventive Activity Revisited*. Chicago, IL: NBER, Chicago University Press, 2012.

D. Foray and B. van Ark, 'Smart Specialisation in a Truly Integrated Research Area is the Key to Attracting more R&D to Europe', in *Knowledge for Growth, European Issues and Policy Challenge*, EUR 23725, European Union, 2008.

D. Foray, P.A. David and B. Hall, 'Smart Specialisation: the Concept', in *Knowledge for Growth: Prospects for Science, Technology and Innovation*, EUR 24047, European Union, 2009.

D. Foray, P.A. David and B. Hall, 'Smart Specialisation: from Academic Idea to Political Instruments, the Surprising Career of a Concept and the Difficulties Involved in its Implementation', Working Paper series, 2011–2001, Management of Technology and Entrepreneurship Institute, EPFL, 2011.

D. Foray and X. Goenega, 'The Goals of Smart Specialisation', *JRC Scientific and Policy Reports*, S3 Policy Brief Series, 01/2013, IPTS, 2013.

D. Foray and F. Lissoni, 'University Research and Public-Private Interactions', in B. Hall and N. Rosenberg (eds), *Handbook of Economics of Innovation*, 1. Amsterdam: North-Holland, 2010.

D. Foray, D.C. Mowery and R.R. Nelson, 'Public R&D and Social Challenges: what Lessons from Mission R&D Programs?', *Research Policy*, 41(10), 2012, pp. 1697–1702.

D. Foray and A. Rainoldi, 'Smart Specialisation Programmes and Implementation', *JRC Scientific and Policy Reports*, S3 Policy Brief Series, 02/2013, IPTS, 2013.

K. Frenken, F. Van Oort and T. Verburg, 'Related Variety, Unrelated Variety and Regional Economic Growth', *Regional Studies*, 41(5), 2007, pp. 685–697.

L. Georghiou, 'The United Kingdom Technology Foresight Programme', *Futures*, 28, 1996, pp. 259–277.

J. Goddard, L. Kempton and P. Vallance, 'Universities and Smart Specialisation: Challenges, Tensions and Opportunities for the Innovation Strategies of European Regions', *Ekonomiaz 83*, II, 2013, pp. 82–101.

B. Hall and J. Lerner, 'Financing R&D and Innovation', in B. Hall and N. Rosenberg (eds), *Handbook in Economics of Innovation*, 1. Amsterdam: North-Holland, 2010.

R. Hausmann and D. Rodrik, 'Economic Development as Self-Discovery', *Journal of Development Economics*, 72, 2003, pp. 603–633.

R. Hausmann, D. Rodrik and A. Velasco, 'Growth Diagnostics', in N. Serra and J. Stiglitz (eds), *The Washington Consensus Reconsidered: Towards a New Global Governance*. Oxford: Oxford University Press, 2008.

F. Hayek, *New Studies in Philosophy, Politics, Economics and the History of Ideas*. London: Routledge and Paul Kegan, 1978.

R. Henderson and I. Cockburn, 'Scale, Scope and Spillovers: Determinants of Research Productivity in the Pharmaceutical Industry', *RAND Journal of Economics*, 27(1), 1996, pp. 32–59.

J.-A. Héraud and R. Lévy, 'University-Industry Relationships and Regional Innovation Systems', in P. Llerena and M. Matt (eds), *Innovation Policy in a Knowledge-based Economy: Theory and Practice*. Berlin: Springer, 2005.

P. Hildreth and D. Bailey, 'The Economics Behind the Move to "Localism" in England', *Cambridge Journal of Regions, Economy and Society*, 6, 2013, pp. 233–249.

J. Hirshleifer, 'The private and social value of information and the reward to inventive activity', *American Economic Review*, 61(4), 1971, pp. 561–574.

A. Houssel and J.P. Houssel, 'L'évolution de la fabrique lyonnaise de soieries', *Revue de Géographie de Lyon*, 67(3), 1992, pp. 187–198.

J. Humphrey and H. Schmitz, 'How Does Insertion in Global Value Chains Affect Upgrading in Industrial Cluster?, *Regional Studies*, 36(9), 2002, pp. 1017–1027.

A. Jaffe, 'Real Effects of Academic Research', *American Economic Review*, 79(5), 1989, pp. 957–970.

A. Jaffe, M. Trajtenberg and R. Henderson, 'Geographic Localization of Knowledge Spillovers as Evidenced by Patent Citations', *The Quarterly Journal of Economics*, 108(3), 1993, pp. 577–598.

M. Kelley and A. Arora, 'The Role of Institution-Building in US Industrial Modernization Programs', *Research Policy*, 25, 1996, pp. 265–279.

S. Kelman, 'The "Kennedy School School" of Research on Innovation in Government', in S. Borins (ed.), *Innovations in Government: Research, Recognition and Replication*. Washington, DC: Brookings Institution Press, 2008.

C. Ketels, 'Recent Research on Competitiveness and Clusters: what are the Implications for Regional Policy?', *Cambridge Journal of Regions, Economy and Society*, 6(2), 2013, pp. 269–284.

I. Kirzner, 'Entrepreneurial Discovery and the Competitiveness Process: an Austrian Approach', *Journal of Economic Literature*, 35(1), 1997, pp. 60–85.

H. Kroll, *Smart Specialisation Approaches – a New Policy Paradigm on its Way from Concept to Practice*, Report, Competence Center Policy and Regions, Fraunhofer Institute for Systems and Innovation Research (ISI), Karlsruhe, 2013.

A. Krueger, 'Comments' in J. Yifu Lin, *New Structural Economics: A Framework for Rethinking Development and Policy*, Washington, DC: World Bank, 2012.

D. Lamb and S. Easton, *Multiple Discovery: The Pattern of Scientific Progress*. Trowbridge: Avebury Publishing Company, 1984.

M. Landabaso, 'The Promotion of Innovation in Regional Policy: Proposals for a Regional Innovation Strategy', *Entrepreneurship and Regional Development*, 9(1), 1997, pp. 1–24.

M. Landabaso, 'Time for the Real Economy: Innovative Strategies for Smart Specialisation and the Need for New Forms of Public Enterprise', draft, 2013.

M. Landabaso and B. Mouton, 'Towards a Different Regional Innovation Policy: 8 Years of European Experience through the European Regional Development Fund Innovative Actions', in M. Van Geenhuizen, D. Gibson and M. Heitor (eds), *Regional Development and Conditions for Innovation in the Network Society*. West Lafayette, IN: Purdue University Press, 2005.

M. Landabaso and A. Reid, 'Developing Regional Innovation Strategies: the European Commission as Animator', in K. Morgan and C. Nauwelaers (eds), *Regional Innovation Strategies: key challenge for Europe's less favoured regions*. London: The Stationary Office, 1999.

J. Lerner, 'The Government as Venture Capitalist: the Long Run Impact of the SBIR Program', *Journal of Business*, 72(3), 1999, pp. 285–318.

P. McCann, 'Globalization and Economic Geography: the World is Curved, not Flat', *Cambridge Journal of Regions, Economy and Society*, 1(3), 2008, pp. 351–370.

P. McCann and R. Ortega-Argilés, 'Smart Specialisation, Regional Growth and Applications to EU Cohesion Policy', *Regional Studies*, 2013a.

P. McCann and R. Ortega-Argilés, 'Modern Regional Innovation Policy', *Cambridge Journal of Regions, Economy and Society*, 6, 2013b, pp. 187–216.

F. Machlup, *Knowledge, its Creation, Distribution and Economic Significance: The economics of information and human capital*, III. Princeton, NJ: Princeton University Press, 1984.

B. Martin, 'Technology Foresight in a Rapidly Globalizing Economy'. Paper presented at the Regional Conference on Technology Foresight, UNIDO, Vienna, 2001.

S. Metcalfe, 'The Economic Foundations of Technology Policy: Equilibrium and Evolutionary Perspectives', in P. Stoneman (ed.), *Handbook of the Economics of Innovation and Technological Change*. Oxford: Wiley-Blackwell, 1995.

S. Metcalfe, 'Capitalism and Evolution', *Journal of Evolutionary Economics*, 24(1), 2014, pp. 11–34.

A. Minkler, 'The Problem with Dispersed Knowledge: Firms in Theory and Practice', *KYKLOS*, 46, 1993, pp. 569–587.

J. Mokyr, *The Gift of Athena: the Historical Origins of the Knowledge Economy*. Princeton, NJ: Princeton University Press, 2004.

K. Morgan, 'The Regional State in the Era of Smart Specialisation', *Ekonomiaz 83*, II, 2013, pp. 102–124.

K. Murphy, A. Shleifer and R. Vishny, 'Industrialization and the Big Push', *The Journal of Political Economy*, 97(5), 1989, pp. 1003–1026.

A. Muscio, L . Rivera Leon and A. Reid, 'Can Smart Specialisation Help Overcome the Regional Innovation Paradox?'. Paper presented at the Conference on the New Structural Economics, UCL-SSEES, London, 2013.

M. Navarro, M.J. Aranguren and E. Magro Montero, 'Smart Specialisation Strategies: the Case of Basque Country', *Orkestra WPseries*, R07, 2011.

F. Neffke, M. Henning and R. Boschma, 'How do Regions Diversify over Time? Industry Relatedness and the Development of new Growth Paths in Regions', *Papers in Evolutionary Economic Geography*, 0916. Utrecht: Utrecht University, 2009.

R.R. Nelson, 'The Simple Economics of Basic Scientific Research', *Journal of Political Economy*, 67, 1959, pp. 297–306.

T. Nikulainen, 'Open Innovation and Nanotechnology: an Opportunity for Traditional Industries', Helsinki: Research Institute of the Finnish Economy, 2008. Available at www.tem.fi/files/25713/Open_Innovation_and_nanotechnology.pdf.

OECD, *Report on Innovation Driven Growth in Regions: the Role of Smart Specialisation*. Paris: OECD, 2012.

M. Percoco, 'Strategies of Regional Development in European Regions: are they Efficient?', *Cambridge Journal of Regions, Economy and Society*, 6(2), 2013, pp. 303–318.

E.S. Phelps, 'Roadblocks to Recovery and Rehabilitation in Global Economy: Crisis without End'. Panel hosted by the *New York Review of Books*, February 17, 2012.

E.S. Phelps, *Mass Flourishing*. Princeton, NJ: Princeton University Press, 2013.

M. Porter, 'Clusters and the New Economics of Competition', *Harvard Business Review*, 76(6), 1998, pp. 77–91.

A. Rodriguez-Clare, 'Coordination Failures, Clusters and Microeconomic Interventions', *IADB Working Paper 544*. Washington, DC: Inter-American Development Bank, 2005.

A. Rodriguez-Pose and R. Dahl Fitjar, 'Buzz, Archipelago Economies and the Future of Intermediate and Peripheral Areas in a Spiky World', *European Planning Studies*, 21(3), 2013, pp. 355–372.

D. Rodrik, 'Industrial Policy for the Twenty-First Century', CEPR, Discussion paper Series, 4767, 2004.

D. Rodrik, 'Normalizing Industrial Policy'. Paper prepared for the Commission on Growth and Development, 2007.

D. Rodrik, 'The Past, Present, and Future of Economic Growth', Global Citizen Foundation, Working Paper 1, 2013a.

D. Rodrik, *Green Industrial Policy*. Princeton, NJ: Institute of Advanced Study, Princeton University, 2013b.

P. Romer, 'Implementing a National Technology Strategy with Self-Organizing Industry Investment Boards', *Brookings Papers on Economic Activity: Microeconomics*, 2, 1993, pp. 345–399.

P. Romer, 'The Arc of Science'. Paper presented at the World Bank Conference, Washington, DC, 2005.

N. Rosenberg, 'The Changing Nature of Medical Technology Development', in N. Rosenberg, A. Gelijns and H. Dawkins (eds), *Sources of Medical Technology: Universities and Industry*. Washington, DC: National Academy of Sciences, 1995a.

N. Rosenberg, 'From the Scalpel to the Scope: Endoscopic Innovations in Gastro-enterology, Gynecology and Surgery', in N. Rosenberg, A. Gelijns and H. Dawkins (eds), *Sources of Medical Technology: Universities and Industry*. Washington, DC: National Academy of Sciences, 1995b.

P. Rosenstein-Rodan, 'Notes on the Theory of the "Big Push"', in H. Ellis and H. Wallich (eds), *Economic Development for Latin America*. New York: St. Martins, 1961.

C. Sabel, *Beyond Principal-Agent Governance: Experimentalist Organizations, Learning and Accountability*. New York: Columbia University Press, 2004.

T. Schlich, *Surgery, Science and Industry – a Revolution in Fracture Care, 1950s-1990s*. Basingstoke: Palgrave Macmillan, 2002.

H. Schmitz and P. Knorringa, 'Learning from Global Buyers,' *IDS Working Paper 1010*, Institute of Develoment Studies, Sussex, 2000.

L. Sopas, The Portuguese mould industry and plastic clusters, 1st meeting of the Portuguese session of the Society of Plastic Engineers, Marinha Grande, 2001.

W.E. Steinmueller, 'Economics of Technology Policy', in B. Hall and N. Rosenberg (eds), *Handbook in Economics of Innovation*, 2. Amsterdam: North-Holland, 2010.

J. Stiglitz and S. Wallsten, 'Public-Private Technology Partnership: Promises and Pitfalls', *The American Behavioral Scientist*, 43(1), 1999, pp. 52–73.

M. Stuetzer, M. Obschonka, U. Brixy, R. Sternberg and U. Cantner, 'Regional characteristics, opportunity perception and entrepreneurial activities', *Small Business Economics*, 42(2), 2014, pp. 221–244.

D. Sull, 'How One Center of Innovation Lost its Spark', *Working Knowledge Series*. Boston, MA: Harvard Business School, 2001.

A. Sumell, P. Stephan and J. Adams, 'Capturing Knowledge: the Location Decision of New PhDs Working in Industry', in R. Freeman and D. Goroff (eds), *Science and Engineering Careers in the United States: An Analysis of Markets and Employment*. Chicago, IL: University of Chicago Press, 2009.

M. Trajtenberg, 'Government Support for Commercial R&D: Lessons from the Israeli Experience', *Innovation Policy and the Economy*, 2, 2002, pp. 79–134.

M. Trajtenberg, 'Innovation Policy for Development: an Overview', in D. Foray (ed.) *The New Economics of Technology Policy*. Cheltenham: Edward Elgar, 2009.

M. Trajtenberg, 'Can the Nelson-Arrow Paradigm still be the Beacon of Innovation Policy?', in J. Lerner and S. Stern (eds), *The Rate and Direction of Inventive Activity Revisited*. Chicago, IL: NBER, University of Chicago Press, 2012.

T. Uotila, V. Harmaakorpi and R. Hermans, 'Finnish Mosaic of Regional Innovation System – Assessment of Thematic Regional Innovation Platform Based on Related Variety', *European Planning Studies*, 20(10), 2012, pp. 1583–1602.

R. Veugelers, 'A Lifeline for Europe's Young Radical Innovators', *Bruegel Policy Brief*, 1, 2009.

R. Veugelers and M. Mrak, 'Catching-up Member States and the Knowledge Economy of the European Union', in *Knowledge for Growth: Prospects for Science, Technology and Innovation*, Report, EUR 24047, European Union, 2009.

R. Weder and H. Grubel, 'The New Growth Theory and Coasean Economics: Institutions to Capture Externalities', *Weltswirtschaftliches Archiv*, 129(3), 1993, pp. 488–513.

R. Wintjes and H. Hollanders, 'Innovation Pathway and Policy Challenges at the Regional Level: Smart Specialisation', *UNU-MERIT working paper series*, 027, 2011.

Index

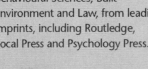

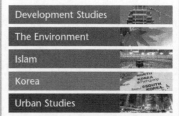